Praise for

Breaking the Cycle of Gang Violence

A moving account of gang-involved youth, *Peace in the Streets* offers a glimpse of the roles that gangs play in the minds of their members, and insight into the potential of these kids, given the proper support. Among Arturo Hernandez's recommendations for communities struggling to cope with gang problems is that efforts to reclaim these children must involve their parents!

Elba Montalvo, executive director,
Committee for Hispanic Children and Families, New York City;
chair, National Council of Latino Executives in Child Welfare;
and member, Board of Directors, Child Welfare League of America

Peace in the Streets gives a vivid and realistic view of the problems that confront Latino youth. It is an important contribution to understanding gang culture and, without being didactic, offers concrete solutions. A great read!

Mary Helen Ponce, professor of literature,
California State University, Los Angeles;
literary reviewer, *Hispanic Magazine;*
and author of *The Wedding* and *Hoyt Street: An Autobiography*

Peace in the Streets offers wisdom and healing for our cities, families, and classrooms. Arturo Hernandez's stories remind us that gang members are our children—no more, no less. This book gives us an alternative, a way to bring our children back from self-destruction.

Dr. Ruben Zacarias, Superintendent,
Los Angeles Unified Schools

PEACE IN THE STREETS

Breaking the Cycle of Gang Violence

Peace in the Streets

Breaking the Cycle of Gang Violence

Arturo Hernandez

Child Welfare League of America
Washington, DC

CWLA Press is an imprint of the Child Welfare League of America, Inc.

The Child Welfare League of America (CWLA) is a privately supported, nonprofit, membership-based organization committed to preserving, protecting, and promoting the well-being of all children and their families. Believing that children are our most valuable resource, CWLA, through its membership, advocates for high standards, sound public policies, and quality services for children in need and their families.

CHILD WELFARE LEAGUE OF AMERICA, INC.
440 First Street NW, Third Floor, Washington, DC 20001-2085
E-mail: books@cwla.org

CURRENT PRINTING (last digit)
10 9 8 7 6 5 4 3 2 1

Cover illustration by Peter Tovar
Cover design by Jennifer R. Geanakos
Text design by Steve Boehm and Jennifer R. Geanakos

Printed in the United States of America

ISBN # 0-87868-692-4

Library of Congress Cataloging-in-Publication Data

Hernandez, Arturo, 1959-
    Peace in the streets : breaking the cycle of gang violence / Arturo Hernandez.
        p. cm.
    ISBN 0-87868-692-4
    1. Gangs--United States--Case studies. 2. Gang members--United States--Rehabilitation. 3. gang members--United States--Psychology, relationships. I. Title.
    HV6439.U5H47 1998
    364.1'06'6'0973--DC21   97-49125
                                                                                            CIP

I dedicate this book to my mother and father,
Ramona and Heladio Hernandez,
for their love, faith, and support without fail;

to the Salt River Pima-Maricopa Indian
Community, Arizona;

and to the boys and girls
of Clanton and Primera Flats, 1982.

Contents

Preface

The 12-year-old wore a white T-shirt and baggy gray work pants. He had cut them at the ankle a few inches so they made a tent over his black high tops. He was about two inches taller than five feet. I sat next to him in the seventh grade dean's office. The chairs were hard, of a dark wood, and had a train station feel to them. He couldn't get comfortable in one. I asked him, "So, what did you do?"

"Nothing. They want to kick me out." He was anxious.

"Is your mother coming?"

No answer.

"So, *qué pasa?* * They bust you doing a *placaso*† on a teacher's butt or something?"

"It's fucked up. The dean says he found a screwdriver in my locker.‡ It's not mine."

"Where do you think they'll send you?"

"I don't know. Probably on the bus somewhere."

"You're gonna have to wake up early."

"I'm not gonna go. Fuck the school."

He went. I don't know how often, or if he went into the new school once he got off the yellow bus, but it was irrelevant. A

---

* What's up, what's happening?

† *Placaso* is gang lingo for one's name in graffiti. The word derives from *placa,* one's gang nickname, and the suffix *-aso,* which implies something akin to "on a grand scale."

‡ Screwdrivers are one way gang members try to get around weapons bans on campus.

couple of weeks after this conversation, he got on the bus, went to the valley, and, instead of going to class, walked over to the corner of a nice residential-commercial block. He waited until a car with local gang members drove by, then he raised his T-shirt and stuck out his belly, with its huge tattoo, "18th Street," across it. They exchanged a few words, the T-shirt stayed up, and the boys in the car took aim with the firearms he knew they would have and tore up his small torso in a few seconds.

This type of suicidal behavior is peculiar to America and, as we all know, is growing beyond our ghettos and consuming greater numbers of our children. I have worked with it for 20 years as a teacher, therapist, community activist, and youth minister. I have come to understand how kids learn to view life with such indifference.

What I am about to share with you is a story that took place in South Central Los Angeles, and, through this story, a difficult but realistic and permanent solution to our nation's gang problem. In 1982, I struck an agreement with the parents and teenagers of Clanton and Primera Flats, two of the oldest neighborhood gangs in East and South Central Los Angeles. The deal created a one-room schoolhouse, where I became the teacher of 30 gang members. The youngest student had recently turned 13; the oldest was almost 20. Both the gang members and their parents knew that I had no teaching credentials or college degree, that I had recently turned 22, and that the school would operate on only a few hundred dollars a month. But we had an idea that we believed in—an idea about what we could do as a neighborhood school raising neighborhood children. To that idea, we added some common sense, a lot of caring, and the help of friends and neighbors.

The gang members in this little school had long histories of truancy, violence, crime, and addiction. Yet for one year, not one student was arrested, was in danger of dropping out, or participated in lethal violence. Surprisingly, this result wasn't that hard to achieve.

I owe the lessons in the first half of this book to the members of the Clanton and Primera Flats gangs, who taught me how much children want to be children, even when they are gang members. The gang members in this book are real people. Only their names have been changed to protect their identities and those of their families.

The second half of the book is based on my experience with gangs in a very different place—the Pima-Maricopa Indian Community on the Salt River Reservation, Arizona. Here, a small desert community struggles with a problem too similar to that in our urban centers. Yet that community's response differs radically from what I have seen in cities across the United States.

I owe the Pima-Maricopa Indian Community a debt for a profound lesson—one that completes the experience I began 20 years ago in South Central Los Angeles. On the Salt River Reservation, I have, for the first time, observed a community take collective responsibility for the problems of its youth. The vision they have adopted aims not only to contain gang violence but to do so in a way that shepherds back the community's most wayward children. The process I am witnessing on this American Indian reservation has inspired much of the advice I offer in the second half of this book.

My most ambitious hope is that this book will help move the dialogue on the gang problem away from one of a war on children to a constructive conversation in which, like the Pima, we sit as a community and decide instead how to heal our most difficult children.

Acknowledgments

Books and their authors survive a long, difficult journey with the help of many friends, only a few of whom I can thank in this space.

Without the skills of my editor, Steve Boehm, and the faith of CWLA Publications Director Sue Brite, this book would have never become a reality. Thank you both.

Without the significant efforts of Martin Orozco to gather a reunion of my old students from El Santo Niño, and without the recollections and advice of Hector Edeza, Carlos Salas, and Johnny Alvarado, much of what is best in this book would not be present.

I owe Todd West and Alexis Navarro for their reading of early manuscripts and careful criticism. In the same regard, I thank Tate Hurvitz, Amy Kern, Araceli Oseguera, and Ryan Leweling for their aid across years of research on this and other projects.

I thank my advisors and teachers at the University of California, Santa Barbara: Professors Mary Brenner, Gale Morrison, Cynthia Hudley-Paul, Yukari Okamoto, Richard Duran, Jules Zimmerman, Jim Block, and Russell Rumberger. Their mentoring strengthened my scholarship and gave direction to much of my thinking. And thanks to Professors Anson Levine, Michael Wapner, and Sy Levitan of California State University, Los Angeles. Their patience, wisdom, and tutelage account for much of my personal and academic accomplishment.

Thank you Nane Alejandrez, founder of Barrios Unidos, for reminding me that I can write because my elders fought.

For making room for my ideas, and for the opportunity to form my gifts, I thank Father Ray Finerty, Father Joe Greenly, Sister Suzanne Jaboro, Sister Natalia Duran, Sister Georgianna, the priests of the Trinitarian Order, the monks at the monastery at Vallermo, Beverly Frank and Dr. Ed Nelson of Catholic Charities, the Brothers of Charity, Father Fitzpatrick of Los Hermanos Unidos, Brother Modesto of the Soledad Enriched Action Schools, and the Theology Department at Loyola Marymount University.

For the bread on my table and for the opportunity to share my experience in their excellent departments, I thank Professors Linda Chaparro of Oxnard City College, Karen Tayback of East Los Angeles City College, and Yvette Flores-Ortiz of University of California, Davis. I am similarly grateful to Frank Gutierrez and George Madrid, directors of P.A.C.E. at East Los Angeles City College. I especially thank all of them for their role in making higher education possible for minority youth.

I also want to thank Steve Saffron, founder of "Humor at Work," for reminding me that laughter heals and for teaching me that "the kid is good"; Franklin Berry, director of education on the Salt River Reservation, for his wide heart and constant welcome; Jervy Tervalon, author of *Understand This,* for his friendship from day one as young teachers at Locke High School, to his generous sharing of advice as I have followed him into the writer's craft; George Wolfe, New York's finest director, who gave me a lasting benchmark for what it means to be an artist; and William Pflueger, mental health activist, for the courage and honesty he has evidenced and for being my best friend since second grade.

To my colleagues, Dale Alpert; Katherine de Anda; Charlene Creeger; Patty Harvey; Julia Howelman; Cheryl Omer; Karen Savitt; Ellie Seidman; Carolyn Stone; and my principal, Kathy Rattay, thank you all for generously sharing your time and experience with me.

I thank the Gestalt Institute of Los Angeles for the financial, intellectual, and emotional support that it has provided me over the years. I am grateful as well to Dr. Earl Henslin for his inspired guidance in the patient art of mending our inner wounds.

And to my brother Marco; my dear friend Earnest Alexander; Tia Concha; William Crane; and Harold, Michelle, and their wonderful kids—thank you for your love and constancy.

I thank my friends Bret, proprietor of Java Jones in Isla Vista; Steve and Marianne of the Isla Vista Cafe; the staff at Anastasia's in Santa Monica; and John, owner of the Onyx in East Hollywood. This book was written in the comfort of their hospitality.

Finally, I owe gratitude to a hardworking, '65 Chevy motor home, which kept me sheltered and rent-free during the years I wrote this book, and to my old brown shepherd, Serena, who kept us safe, snored under the writing table, and shared a very long walk with me.

Introduction

The Beach Boys went to my high school. We moved into their neighborhood after the Watts riots, when African Americans, Caucasians, Latinos, Asian Americans—when everyone in the city—picked up and went somewhere else to be with their own kind. There was no trace of the Beach Boys left in Highland Park as brown folks cleared escrow and white folks packed themselves into station wagons and fled.

This created a new Mexican neighborhood, and I saw the first gang form on my street. First Hooknose, whose father fixed our cars, started ditching school along with Cantu, who lived two blocks down from me and would never open his mouth in class, even to go to the bathroom. The two always hid in the tunnel to scare elementary school kids, or took lunch money from students on their way to junior high.

In junior high school, this duo immediately met other young teens of similar circumstances—kids with nothing but time on their hands, who had trouble in school such that they cared little about poor report cards, homework, detention, or suspension. They had little to plan their days around except for the chores that mom needed done and the mischief they could conjure up.

Hooknose and Cantu had found a group like themselves to hang out with for ditching parties, access to drugs and alcohol, and general carousing. Soon, they were calling themselves the "Highland Park Gang" and writing "HLP" on local walls; stealing things; joyriding in stolen cars; and, pretty much for the hell of it, getting into fights with similar groups in adjacent neighborhoods.

I knew all the HLP parents. Since ethnic groups tend to move together, most of their parents immigrated from the same cluster of villages as my parents. None of the parents were gang members, and most of the families were Catholic, two-parent households. Some were better parents than others, but that's true of any group.

When the gang formed, it wasn't with the intention of becoming a "gang." This bunch of kids hung out together because they had things in common, including a dislike of school. Of course, they also had no intention of becoming addicts or ending up in jail or ruining their lives. But 14-year-olds don't think that far ahead. It sort of snuck up on them.

I was never invited to become part of this group, even though I knew them all. I didn't like the khakis they wore, the '50s oldies they listened to, being high all the time, or spending my days at the park just bullshitting. I did like Paul Simon, playing the guitar, and reading. The new *cholos** had plenty of adventures I enjoyed hearing about; but I had my own adventures, and the price for their kind exceeded my desire to participate.

No one ever got forced in. Kids, like all people, want to hang out with others whose company they enjoy. When someone got jumped into the gang it was because both sides were looking forward to it.

My brother, my best friend, and I were the only kids on the block who didn't participate in anything more than porch banter with our local "gang." My brother entertained himself by practicing martial arts, which eventually led him to an acting career. My best friend and I got busy becoming musicians. Those interests gave us long-term peer groups, goals, and a daily occupation. But each of us came to these pursuits by pure chance. My brother because he befriended some Korean students and became fascinated with Bruce Lee films; myself

---

*   Gang members.

because I suffered a leg disease, which kept me at home most of the time; and my best friend because he learned guitar after I taught him some chords and gave him my sheet music.

What did the parents of the HLP gang try on their behalf? Just about everything they knew to do. They punished their kids, talked to them, locked them in the house. None of these approaches were very effective. Sending them to Mexico proved worthwhile when possible. A 14-year-old who did not succeed in school simply joined the work force in Mexico.

This is not an argument for child labor, but we should be aware that there is no plan B in this country when plan A fails. We don't know how to make school work for all kids, especially minority kids, and we don't provide alternatives. If a kid is not in school and doesn't have anything of particular importance to take the place of school, the only thing left is mischief.

I learned a bit more about gangs in the seventh grade.

I naively took electric shop, and I took it seriously, reading books and trying to build crystal radios. This annoyed my shop teacher, who liked to teach students to build wooden light boxes that required a minimal explanation of electricity. Shop teachers spend their days with the students no one else wants and who can't pass anything else.

Once a week, the teacher gave a quiz based on our shop textbook. It may have been a requirement of the school district, or maybe one of his conscience. Few students came to class on that day, and those who did waged war the whole period. I don't remember any student capable of reading through the shop textbook except for myself. The teacher hated reading day, the other students hated it, and I hated it.

Sometimes, the older gang members in class would take my pocket change, but not too often. Over time, a distant respect arose between us, and an understanding on my part. These were loser kids. There was no other way to put it. They had no business being in a school that did nothing but shame them. I could not imagine one of these guys taking home a history or algebra book, working through the chapter, and coming to class the next day with work neat and complete. Over the course of

the year, some stopped coming to school, others provoked
expulsions, and a few finished the year in juvenile hall. I
watched them drift off one at a time, week after week.

This moved me. I had spent my junior high years trying to
compensate for a physical handicap that kept me separate from
the activities of my friends. I understood the pain of wanting to
be something besides what I was. A similar sentiment existed
among the gang members with whom I interacted daily. They
constantly chided each other over who was the worst failure,
and although it was funny, it was also hard. "I'm not going to
live to be 20, so who cares?" This sentence inevitably came up as
the last defense of failure, addiction, or some destructive act
whenever gang members argued.

Through music, I found a bridge to acceptance, a place in the
world. But what provided this bridge for the gang members I
talked with in shop class? Drugs, fighting, acting crazy? Such
activities gave them status with each other, but the world
outside their group remained unimpressed, and they couldn't
ignore this. I remember standing next to Wizard. We were
soldering wires on a circuit board. He told me: "I want to join the
Marines. I always think about that man in a black suit coming
to my mom's house and telling her I died in a war, for my
country, you know? That would be the first time my mom would
ever be proud of me."

My mother made a point of picking up every injured pigeon,
dog, or neighbor's child and bringing it home. She taught us not
to ignore the suffering of others. As soon as I could drive, I asked
my pastor, Father Greenly, if he would allow me to work on the
juvenile hall visitation team. What I learned in the detention
facility rounded out the lessons of the electric shop.

In detention, the inmates became both sorry and motivated.
Incarceration had the desired effect: It made them reconsider
their situations and kindled in them intentions to do better. But
once they were released, their resolutions met the resistance of
old habits, old friends, inexperience, and inability. For the next
two years, I tried an experiment at my church that I thought
might help gang members hold onto their better convictions.

Father Greenly helped me organize a team of adult and teen volunteers. From the pulpit, he asked if families in the parish would be willing to mentor the neighborhood boys and girls who would soon be released from incarceration. This mentorship would be an aid to the parents of these inmates—a second family, or *compadres,* as we say in Spanish. Teenagers usually prefer adult advice to be delivered by someone other than their own parents.

The teens who volunteered served as a peer support group—friends to get the released gang members involved in church activities, sports, and other salubrious pursuits. Both teen and adult volunteers tutored students and generally encouraged school success. Our experiment was brief. After one year, I discontinued it when college demands forced a choice between volunteer activities and passing classes. But one year proved enough time to succeed with a few kids. The cost? Plenty, in terms of time, labor, and patience. At no point, however, did it take genius on our part—only unwavering constancy and high-octane energy.

This experience clarified for me that gang-involved kids needed an adult world—not just their parents, but a whole community of adults. Together, we could teach them not only what wrongs to avoid but also what they were supposed to be doing right. More than lecturing, gang-involved teens needed to learn how to read, do homework, stay sober, play a guitar, or apply for a job. They needed strong supervision to keep them from straying, and lots of rewards to keep them going.

And they needed time. The community could not give up on them after a few months or because a single program didn't straighten them out. Shortcuts didn't exist in this arena. Unfortunately, one year could only begin a process. These kids still had lots of growing up to do, and they needed special help with it the whole way through. As good as I felt about what we accomplished, I dismantled the program knowing that we left these kids without the railing that they still needed to hold onto.

About four years later, just after I turned 21, I took a position as an aide at Adams Junior High School in South Central Los

Angeles. Besides coordinating a volunteer project with a neigh-boring university, the job required that I assist the truancy counselor on home visits. That's how I first met the young members of the Clanton and Primera Flats gangs and made a promise to create a place for them.

PART ONE

SIX GANG MEMBERS
TEACH ME
THAT IT TAKES
A VILLAGE

Huero Dies at the Laundramat

"*Y como andan tus cholos?*" *

My father was making his usual breakfast of *chicharónes,* †
fried tortillas, refried beans, and a special chili made from the
leftover fat ladled over the whole thing. My mother had some
French toast.

"They're out of control," he told me. "The Avenues are
finishing off the boys from Highland Park. Yesterday they killed
El Huero." Huero was 14 and a regular at County General
Hospital, where cholos have their bullets extracted.

Everyone in the neighborhood remembered how, years ago,
a cholo had been shot at the door of my father's coin laundry, the
Monte Vista Laundramat,‡ and was soaking in a blood pool.
People were watching, waiting for the police. Then 7-year-old
Huero broke through the crowd on his bicycle and made red
circles with his tires in the dying boy's blood. Round and round
the new GE washers.

Now, my father told me how, yesterday, Huero and his
brother Poncho had been walking down Monte Vista Street
when Poncho saw a carload of "Avenues" at the stop. Poncho,
who had a metal leg, was the neighborhood mail-order thief. He

---

*   "And how are your cholos doing?"

†   Refried pork fat.

‡   *Laundromat,* with an "o," is a service mark for a type of self-serve coin-
operated laundry. Not to be confused with that chain, my father's coin
laundry was called the Laundramat, with an "a."

would ride around on his bicycle, with his leg banging a steady rhythm everyone recognized. He would take orders on a little paper from his pocket for televisions, car stereos, or toys. Then he would go to the local stores and steal those things, showing up in a day or two with the merchandise. He was frequently caught and would disappear for months at time.

The leg itself was a gift from the county, who attached it after a passing shotgun and a prolonged beating had severed the real one. "All homeboys been shot in the legs. Bullets go down, that's why you have to run." Poncho had offered me that bit of wisdom in case anyone ever took a gun to me.

Poncho hopped across the street into the Monte Vista Arms apartments. He started calling out for other Highland Park boys, quite a few of whom slept on the roof of the apartment building. The boys had once told my father that if the Russians ever decided to take Highland Park, the gang could hold off the invaders. *"Tenemos bala para buen rato,"* they told him. "We have bullets to last for a good long while."

Huero didn't follow Poncho. Instead, he stood there and exchanged hand signs with the Avenues and then sped off, running through the Laundramat. The Avenues pulled through the alley and caught him in the parking lot, carved him up, and draped him over the fence. It all took very little time. Huero's mother, who lived two doors down, hurried to the Laundramat with neighbors who heard the fight.

"What else did you expect?" my father asked her. His cynicism came from a time when Huero was 10. The boy had written all over the Laundramat and then confessed when caught with the markers. The mother had immediately broken in, "How do you know it was my son?"

"Señora, the boy admitted it. It's good that he be honest."

She had looked at her son and barked, "Why are you telling people that you do these things?"

Since then, my father had blamed her for the boy's troubles, but his judgment wasn't fair. Her three boys were hard to keep up with, and she spent too much time apologizing for them. Sometimes she just tired of it. She spent most of her days

chasing them around, bailing them out of jail, trying to get a
new school to take them.

For her son, Spooky, at least, we had all thought there might
be a chance. The whole neighborhood remembered him as the
tamale man's son. He used to sit on the corner with his father,
next to the hot aluminum barrel, and quote Bible verses to
customers. He was cute. But Spooky had gotten a pipe to his
head the day his parents had bailed him out last year. And now
El Huerito was gone too.

So that morning before work, I went with my father into his
tool room and watched him make another little cross out of wire
and old machine parts. He walked outside and tied the metal
cross to a long water pipe that ran the length of his coin laundry.
My father put the new cross next to the one he had made for
Spooky. Everyone knew he placed these in the alley whenever
a local boy died. People occasionally put flowers on them.

* * * * *

*Most gang members have parents who love them. That is seldom the
problem. But some children need help beyond what a loving parent can
offer. That's what the rest of us are here for. What I enjoy about Native
American communities is that you don't have to convince them of this.*

Losing Shorty

He was shy, soft-voiced, adrift, schooled but without effect—a brown, moonfaced boy with doe-like eyes that girls found really cute. He looked more like 13 than 16. Shorty hadn't passed a class his whole eighth and ninth grade years. Because of his age, the junior high would advance him to high school in September, but I doubted he would attend classes.

If Shorty had a job, that would be the best thing, I thought. I could help him get one, and then I could help get jobs for other gang members. I wanted to do more than just chase these kids around the neighborhood with the truancy counselor.

I met Nemo, Shorty's older brother, on Friday, when they came by the school in Nemo's white, early '60s pickup. Nemo was a hefty boy with cropped hair and deliberate speech. He didn't exert too much energy, but he was willing to talk.

"Nice truck. What year?" I asked Nemo as I leaned into the passenger window.

"1962 Chevy."

"Are you going to fix it up?"

"I'm going to lower it and put on some rims. I got a shotgun hidden under my seat so no one fucks with it."

"You just waiting for the money?"

"I got the money. I told Shorty to work for me, but he's stupid. It's that *ruca** that's bumping his head. I got Violet and

---

* Girl.

Sylvia [their 7-year-old twin sisters] making more money than this fool." He paused. "Just fucking with you, Shorty."

"What do your sisters do?" I asked Shorty.

"Is this guy a narc or something?" Nemo asked Shorty. He really didn't seem that worried about it.

Ignoring Nemo, Shorty told me, "They take Nemo's stuff around to different people, or people come around to them while they pretend they're playing."

"Cops are stupid," Nemo added. "They're always pulling me over thinking I'm gonna have shit on me."

They left for home in the truck. Later that week, I heard there had been a killing at the L.A. Street Scene, the yearly festival along Broadway, in the heart of Los Angeles. The papers reported that a gang member had walked up to a truck and killed the guy at the wheel. When I saw Shorty, who was hanging out a lot in the truancy office, he brought it up.

"You heard about my brother?"

"Was that him? What happened, man?" I pulled him up a chair so we could sit close.

"He was parked at the L.A. Street Scene downtown and some guy came up to the window—he had it open—and the guy just fired on him and took off. I called my mom, and she says they can't show his body cause his face is all messed up."

"Have you seen your mother?"

"No, not yet."

"I made plans to take you job hunting tomorrow. If you want, we can also go by to see your mom. Do you still want to look for a job?"

"Yeah, I still do."

The next morning, I went to pick him up where he and his girlfriend, Nikki, were staying. They had moved in together a month earlier, after she had gotten pregnant. That was another reason I didn't think he would finish school. Lynwood, where Nikki lived, was once a white suburb that called itself "America's town." After the Watts riots, real estate agents canvassed the area, "block busting," to get people to sell by instilling fear that "Negroes from the riots are taking over." They drove carloads of

African Americans through the neighborhoods and spread rumors. The result was a lot of quick commissions and cheap deals for agents and their clients, who wanted income property.

Another result was a chaotic city and unregulated growth. Renters replaced homeowners, dairy farms sold their small fields to developers, and the rural feel of the city disappeared along with its spotted cows. The main street, Imperial Highway, became cluttered with cheap motels catering to hookers. It became a street that made you nervous at red lights and stop signs.

Shorty and his girlfriend were living in one of these motels. The rent took up the entire welfare check for Nikki's 3-year-old, and food stamps kept them from starving. The room was brown—brown curtains, brown walls, brown covers, brown nightstand. There was no air conditioning, the heat kept the toddler in a constant rash, and the crying had them sleepless.

On the slow ride along the Long Beach Freeway—always jammed, since it's a truck route and there's always some kind of spill—he told me how he had been making extra money and that he had seen the president.

"I saw President Reagan."

"Where was this?"

"We were in Beverly Hills knocking over parking meters."

"And you saw the president?"

"There were all these people on the end of the street, so I went to check it out, and the president was driving by in his car."

"Man, weren't you afraid of getting busted? Beverly Hills has a lot of police."

"You do it really fast and someone follows in a car so you can just jump in."

"How much did you make?"

"About $200, but we had to split it with everybody in the car, so I got $30. I gave it to Nikki for the baby."

We got off at Macy Street, where all the big junk yards are. We drove past Union Station and Olvera Street, where Macy becomes Sunset Boulevard and divides Chinatown from downtown. The Music Center was showing something new at the

Ahmanson, and I could see some of the orchestra members in black suits carrying their cases of strange and assorted geometry.

We were in Echo Park–Silverlake in a few minutes. I parked and walked with Shorty to the two-story apartment building where his mother lived. When we knocked, she hollered, "Who is it?" and then told us to come in when Shorty answered her. As we did, she walked out of her bathroom and met us. She was a 36-year-old with a thin figure and bleached streaks in her brown hair. She had a teenage quality about her, dressed in cords, Hush Puppies, and a T-shirt.

"I'm sorry about Nemo. I met him just the other day. He was a good guy." What else could I say?

"Nemo was my man. I know he was bad, but he supported this family. Everyday this week, the devil's been after me. He waits under my bed and shakes it. I know Jesus will protect me. This morning, the devil was shaking my bed, and I thought the babies could hear him, and I screamed, 'Jesus is with me!' That made him stop."

"That's good. You've got courage." I didn't know what else to say.

"Shorty knows I'm not afraid. And I'm not one of those moms that's old-fashioned. They don't got anything they can pull on me. Help Shorty out. I've got my hands full, and I know something's happening to me since they killed Nemo. I just want to find the fuck that did this and make him feel what I feel. I know it isn't right to feel that way."

Back on the street I asked Shorty about his dad. "He died from a motorcycle accident. He and my mom used to ride together, but then he got hit and kept getting sick. That's when Nemo started dealing."

I bought Shorty a shirt at the Lynwood thrift and a $25 suit that fit him like Charlie Chaplin's in *The Little Tramp*. He looked like a cartoon character. I had a letter on school stationery explaining that he was a good kid in a special program and that we would appreciate an employer giving him a chance. An Asian man at the Lakewood Mall read the letter and said he would work something out. He taught Shorty how to stock and sell the shoes, and paid him a few dollars a day under the table. He really didn't need the help, so it was mainly to help out. It wasn't enough money though, and Shorty wanted to try something else by the end of the first week.

We went to the Arby's at the end of the mall parking lot, and the owner, an older white man, looked at the letter and said he would interview him. "Let's say a Coke costs 68¢, and you get a dollar. Count back the change to me."

Nothing. Shorty's eyes just froze. He couldn't do it on paper either. He just had no idea.

"Look, I want to help you Robert," the owner said, using Shorty's given name, "but I can't have you at the register if you can't make change, and all our employees work all the stations. You have to cook, make change, take orders, and clean."

"What if I can teach him?" I offered. "Can he come back?"

"If he can learn this, I'd be willing to give him a chance."

We worked on it for a week, counting money forward, backward, and sideways. He picked up the idea at the end of the first day, and by the week's end he was on a cruise with it. We went back, and the man stuck to his word and gave Shorty the job. But he only lasted five weeks because he had difficulty being on time. He wasn't used to it, the baby kept him up at night, the buses were slow to come again if he missed one, and he got hassled by other gang members because of the black tear tattooed under his eye—signifying he had spent time in jail. Besides the tattoo, his hair cut, clothes, and mannerisms gave him away as a gang member. For Shorty, this meant continuous confrontation on the buses he took across gang territories.

"Can't I go back to school?" he asked me. "I feel like that's what I should be doing."

"Where would you live? And how about Nikki?"

I felt conflicted about my response. Father Sharp at St. Vincent's, who baptized Nikki's baby, had already warned me not to encourage Shorty and Nikki to get married. "Don't pile another problem on these kids." It wasn't so much that I wanted them to get married, or Shorty on the career track at

Arby's, but resources had thinned out at my end, and I just wanted him established somewhere.

Shorty replied, "Maybe I can go home, and she can live with her mom again. I don't know, but I'm going to get fired and I keep thinking about school."

"You've got to decide something," I said. "Maybe you can go to the Job Corps like your friend David. I'm getting busy, and it's getting hard for me to take you around like this."

"I know you aren't always going to be around."

He was right. We lost touch with each other a short time after that conversation. It was one of many lessons for me in the uselessness of being the Lone Ranger, Mr. Ghetto Warrior. No kid should have his survival hinging on just one person, and no single adult should have to be the only source of help.

* * * * *

On my father's farm, it was custom for a boy to sleep with his herd as it traveled across the arid Mexican highlands. In the summer, long after the last rains, cattle wandered for days in search of disappearing grasses.

Nights held danger. Wolves and mountain lions hunt best in the hedge of twilight. So, as evening fell, the cows naturally assembled into a circle, and the young herdsman would camp in its center, snuggling amidst the calves. The bulls that accompanied the herd walked the perimeter throughout the night, scaring away predators.

It took many cows and vigilant bulls to make the circle in which calves and herder found protection. Wolves were always waiting for the one too lost or weak to make it back at the end of the day.

Silent Desperation

I buttoned my long, black coat to the top. It felt good and thick. "Made of real Tijuana snake skin," my mother quipped when my father bought it at the border. I kicked over the engine on my Honda 450, and the growling mufflers launched me into high orbit, like a well-shot marble out of Highland Park.

My trench coat started flapping at the ends; cold, night jasmine rushed through the helmet. I twisted back the throttle and flew over Dodger Stadium, downshifted, and fell into Chinatown, where the air smelled good and fat in the steam of ginger, spicy noodles, and chicken fried rice. Stone Chinese dragons sat on restaurant doorways and lined the pointy roofs. They leapt off their perches like loose dogs and ran me out to Sunset and Alameda, to the corner of Olvera Street, where the best taquitos in the world sang in three inches of *manteca.** As I stood to order, I thought about the salty, hot green *tomatillo* sauce and how I'd lick it off the wax paper, chase it with a Coke, and pant through the afterburn.

I cruised a few blocks along Alameda, the rail moat separating East L.A. from downtown, and turned up First Street. I came in for a landing on the winos' end of Main Street. The sidewalks moved about as the ragged people stuffed newspapers in their shirts and pants for warmth; made cardboard beds; and drank, slept, watched, and argued. The January night seemed to yawn wide on skid row.

---

* Lard.

I cut my engine and backed up with my feet. Straight ahead, a heavy woman in canary-yellow hot pants sat comfortably on a fire hydrant. She was hollering and waving at traffic, grabbing guys by the elbow as they passed, calling them "honey." I parked in front of the tattoo shop and asked the owner as I dismounted, "How much do you think she gets?"

He didn't answer right away. Maybe he was thinking. Then he said, "Some guys will pay $15 for a woman like that." Maybe he was one of those guys, so I shut up. I walked to the corner to avoid her. Pushy people embarrass me. I entered the same brick building I had visited twice in the last week and walked toward the yellow light at the turn of the stairs.

Except for the Alexandria Hotel—big and decent with a club on the first floor where Latinos brought their boots and ranchero hats to *taconear** in style—the hotels on skid row, with their faded tattoos announcing, "Modern singles, fireproof and furnished," were built 50 years ago for rail and truck workers; unloaders of fish, vegetables, furniture, and live pigs; mechanics; cooks; and janitors. Mexican families now lived in these hotels, and they had children who needed to be in school.

At the top of the stairs, a young man read a magazine in his wire cage. His job required him to keep out transients and to rent out rooms. *CHiPs* showed on his little TV, and a tiny Erik Estrada was biking around. I moved past him along the bare wood floor and knocked on door 6.

"Who are you?" A small, thin boy with an amaretto complexion stared back at me, waiting for my answer. He wore gray, wide khakis, pressed and creased; an oversized, blue and gray Pendleton wool shirt, buttoned to the collar; a black hair net positioned so that the seams formed a dark spider over his brow; and pointy, polished, black Imperials on his feet. Unmistakably cholo.

"I work for Adams Junior High. Are you Eugenio?"

"Are you Eugenio?" he mimicked my question without taking his eyes off me. I noticed he had a small tattoo between

---

*   From *tacón,* the heel of a shoe, *taconear* literally means to click or stomp one's heels. In this contect, *taconear* is dancing or "heel stomping."

his thumb and forefinger that spelled "Silent." I tried that instead.

"Silent. I need to see your mother or father. You haven't been to school in quite a while."

He looked back at a woman coming toward the door and muttered, *"Leva,"*[†] as he walked past me and down the hall. My stomach tightened at the vague threat.

I told the woman approaching me, "I think I just angered your son. I'm with the truancy office at Adams."

"I'm sorry. Don't pay attention to him. Do you want to come in? We weren't expecting anyone. Please, come in." She opened the door wider and stepped aside to let me in. "Would you like a taco?" she asked while leading me through a clean and well-appointed living room with *The Last Supper* hanging over a sand-colored couch.

A few tacos lay warm and still on the kitchen stove. "Yes, if it isn't too much trouble. The cold makes me hungry, and it smells good in here." We moved into the kitchen and sat at the Formica table. A white plate with intricate blue trim moved from the stove towards me.

"Gracias, señora. I hate coming to people's homes at night like this. But there are so many kids the truant counselor and myself can't find during the day. I'm his assistant."

"Está bien," she answered. "That's all right. I'm just embarrassed that you have to do this for my boys."

"Quien es, mija?"[‡] came a man's voice from the living room. "Who is it?"

"Es de la escuela de los muchachos," she answered. "He is from the boys' school."

[†]   *Leva* is a cholo expression that isn't even Chicano slang but cholo slang. "You'll get yours" is as close as one can get to an English translation, although "Watch your back" is also implied. Often used among gang members, the term always implies that the recipient is in for a hard time.

[‡]   *Mija* and *mijo* are shortened forms of *mi hija* and *mi hijo,* literally meaning "my daughter" or "my son." Spouses often use these as terms of endearment between each other.

A tall, older man with deep lines in his face, a tight T-shirt, and black pants came into the kitchen. She pointed him towards me as I stood up to meet the father of the house.

"I thought the boy's were here," he said to his wife.

"Eugenio left when he saw the man at the door. I don't know where Alfredo went."

The man sat down. His wife made a plate for him as well and brought a can of Pepsi and a dish of yellow peppers from the refrigerator. I wasn't sure where to start, so I waited for the mother to join us before saying anything. No one seemed to be either uncomfortable or impressed about my being here.

"I just started these night visits," I explained. "The counselor is an older man, so he only works in the day. We've come by here a couple of times, but no one answers."

"Its complicated," Silent's mother told me. Both she and her husband hesitated.

"Maybe I can help?"

"I wish you could," she said. "With Alfredo I still have hope. Eugenio, I don't know. I wish someone could take him away to a military academy. I sleep better when the police have him detained."

"I can tell that Eugenio can be stubborn." I slipped my arms out of my trench coat to lay it back over the chair. It didn't feel professional.

"Alfredo is more noble, but he follows his younger brother," she said. "He wants to be an artist. That's part of the reason we opened our business. My father gave me the money to open a T-shirt printing store. Alfredo works with me there. But he won't go to school. The problem is that the school won't let him work without a permit, and they say they'll report me." She looked at me. I could tell that my being with the school district didn't automatically make me helpful in this case. The only way for Alfredo to get a work permit was to be in school.

"I have nothing to do with that. Maybe I can talk to somebody. Sometimes there are ways to do things."

"*Por favor,* if you can do anything, because at work at least I can watch him. And he works hard."

"And Silent?"

The father looked straight at me. "He told you to call him that?"

"At the door, when he was on his way out, I noticed the tattoo. He wouldn't answer to Eugenio."

"These boys have no respect for themselves or anyone else," he lamented into the kitchen air.

The mother was sitting to my right, and she appeared pained. She was thinking, maybe wondering how far she should go into this with me.

"Eugenio's in a gang?" I asked. The question was a gambit, but one based on what I had seen when he opened the door.

Silent's mother needed no prompting to answer the obvious. "Both my sons are cholitos, but Eugenio's the worst. Alfredo goes to the parties on the weekends, but he comes to work and respects me. Eugenio I have no control over."

"Since when?"

"Even as a baby he was difficult," she said. "When we came to Los Angeles, we had to leave him with my sister in Sonoita for a while. I don't know how much that had to do with it, but he has always been angry, stubborn. He's always fought with teachers. They've kicked him out of every school he's gone to."

"I should have let you take him to Mexico," the father added. "My wife wanted to return with the children and live with her parents, but I wanted her here with me. I had no idea what was coming. I'm sorry now."

"Does Eugenio also work at the T-shirt store with you?"

"I don't like him there." Her voice softened into a monotone. "He takes the paints and uses them to drug himself. He's no help at all. I really have no answer anymore. He listens to no one, and I'm afraid one day he'll hurt his grandparents when he's angry."

I sensed the fear in the house. And the shame. I had no answer either.

"This is very hard," I said, my own voice softer and slower. "I'll see about Alfredo tomorrow. Let me think about Eugenio. I know you are ready to give up, but sometimes a new person, someone who isn't a parent, can reach a teenager."

"Let's hope it is that way," Silent's father responded.

"Is there a time when Eugenio is here?"

With her hand on her face, she gave me a small head motion for no. "I know they go to a house full of gang members over by the school. The boys call it 'the Mansion.' I don't know why the police don't close that place or burn it down. I don't know who owns it, but they sleep there and from what I hear do whatever they want. My husband has tried to follow the boys, we've called the police, but. . . ." Her hands lifted slightly off the table as she failed to finish the sentence.

"I think if I ask around the school I can find that house. I'm sure many of the kids know about it. Let me see, and we'll talk again. I have the school on my side. The police listen to them. If there is anything else I can do, please call me at Adams." I put on my coat as I stood up. "It's a rough street outside."

"It's not that bad," the father said. "The drunks don't hurt anyone, and you don't hear gunshots like you do in other parts of the city. We know the owner of these apartments, so the rent is very low." He added, "We could save money in this country—something impossible where we came from. But we paid another price."

I thanked them for the tacos and for their hospitality. I shook the father's hand, but the mother just stood there as I went out the door. This was a strange visit, and I felt both a little tired and a little wired. It had gotten colder, and I wished I had someone to call and have a late coffee with me.

Marisela

E d Scanlan, counselor for the truancy office, had once been a priest, lastly at Blessed Sacrament in Hollywood. He left after 30 years. He told me it had been difficult to live within the expectations. Which ones, he didn't offer. He was kind, without intention of marrying, and respectful of the church. He had just bought a car with $10,000 cash. We rode around in it. He did most of the talking; I did all of the chasing and translating.

Kids liked getting chased. Usually, Mr. Scanlan would drive up next to them, open the door lock, and let me go. We'd run through alleys, around corners, through auto repair yards, and then the kid would turn around, slow up, and wait to get caught. I'd have a sweaty eighth grader in a one-armed hug, and he'd be both laughing and acting mad.

"Let me go Hernandez, or I'm gonna sock you."

I never got socked. The boys knew I would never chase them again, and there would go the afternoon adventures. When you ditch school all the time, it gets pretty boring around midday. A good chase when you're 13 years old just hits the spot.

It was Monday morning, and Mr. Scanlan and I had started our rounds in his new Buick.

"My friends think it was stupid to take all my savings and buy a car," he said. "Arturo, this is probably the last car I will ever own. I've never had payments, certainly not as a priest." He showed me a list of the homes we had to visit this morning.

"You have perfect handwriting," I noted.

"It was Catholic school. The nuns made us do circles and circles. They don't teach that anymore. I think it was valuable." He drove slowly, a grandfatherly, tall gentleman in a sensible car. The Buick gave a nice ride, and it gave us time to talk.

Our first visit on this particular morning was to the northeast side of USC, on a street with student housing on one side and the ethnic swell reaching high tide on the other. This week, two coeds had been attacked by 15-year-old gang members who had decided to rape as an initiation, and the campus paper was advising women to stay on their side of the moat.

The Victorian homes in this area had been subdivided into rooming houses, so you never knew who would answer the hallway door. At our address, the girl we were sent to find actually answered the chime. She hadn't been to school in several months.

Several months is usually how long it took us to make a home visit, even with monitoring attendance by computer. Kids intercepted calls and mail, forged notes, and hid report cards and letters. They knew which period's attendance went to the school attendance office, and they would attend that class so that the attendance records would make it look like they were in school. By the time cases got to a special counselor, who had several thousand kids in a couple of schools, the student may have been out of school for a long time. Even then, what? The police weren't going to escort the kid to school—skipping school wasn't really a crime. And if you succeeded in getting the kid back to school, the teachers hated you. What were teachers supposed to do with angry, lost kids who only showed up once a week and had no idea what was going on in class? But there we were.

Marisela (a pretty name, I thought) brought a chair from the kitchen for herself. She pulled down on her knit blue miniskirt, which matched her halter and eye shadow. She was a pale, meaty girl with streaked blond hair. Her mother sat on a dark green lounger. She was not old, but she was small, wrinkled, and tired. Like moms we found everywhere—in Van Nuys, Pico-

Union, Hollywood, the East Side—she seemed exhausted, without a clue as to why her children didn't do what others did, having little to offer except an apathetic politeness. She understood her daughter had been ditching, looked at her, looked at us, back at her.

I went through the usual questions, asking in Spanish, "And why haven't you been to school, Marisela?"

"I don't know. I don't like it. I'd rather work."

"What does your daughter do for work, Señora?"

"She helps a man sell jewelry."

I told Mr. Scanlan the girl was selling jewelry for a man instead of coming to school. Scanlan told Marisela it was good that she worked, but she would have to come back to school. It was the law for a 14-year-old. We would expect her in the morning. I translated to Marisela's mother. Her perfunctory, "I understand," made me uneasy.

Mr. Scanlan saw that I appeared to be waiting for more in her reply. "Do you want to talk to her for a little while, Arturo?"

"I think there's more that we don't understand, Mr. Scanlan. I'd like to ask her if she wants Marisela to go to school. She doesn't really seem enthusiastic for the idea." Marisela listened to this but didn't seem concerned about my intent to probe a bit. Scanlan made himself comfortable.

By now, I had noticed a small tattoo on Marisela's ankle. Peeking out of her shoe when she bounced her foot, it spelled "HARPYS" in small, Old English lettering, the kind favored by gangs in this area. The small Harpys gang roamed a section of tenements to one side of USC, but its members lived tenuously between the monster 18th Street gang to the west and the older Clanton, Primera Flats, and Diamond Street gangs to the east.

I now had questions for both Marisela and her mother. "Señora, I sense that there might be a reason that Marisela is better off at work. I noticed the tattoo on her foot." I pointed to the tattoo, and still Marisela only stared back at me.

Her mother also stared toward me for a few moments. She appeared to be organizing her thoughts, choosing words. She replied in a voice still quiet, but with conviction and impatience in her tone, "She is not a bad girl, but she does nothing at school except get together with those cholitos. I gave her a choice, and she chose work. At least I know where she is all day. I can take her to your school every morning, but can you guarantee that someone will know where she is or that she won't leave to be on the street? I know you can't. I also know that if she gets into any trouble, you're going to send her to schools far from here, and how will that help? I can barely keep my eye on her here. How can I if she is in some school further away? It doesn't make sense, does it?"

She looked at Mr. Scanlan for a moment and then back toward me. She still had a little more to say. "If I'm going to spend my days going to meetings at the school that don't result in anything, I might as well have her with me. If you can't offer some solution to this girl's problem, then let me handle it my way." Her eyes were locked onto me. I'm sure she had rehearsed this speech from the day she let Marisela stop attending school.

I told Mr. Scanlan what Marisela's mother had said. His reply didn't soothe me, but it contained all the facts: "Arturo, the law states that she has to be in school. We'll try to get some help for her, but, no, we can't guarantee anything. Let her know we'll be back, and we'll put some thought into this. But we do expect her in the morning."

I translated this to Marisela's mother as carefully and without threat as I could. Mr. Scanlan then asked Marisela if she understood, and she answered a very polite, "Yes."

In the car, while Scanlan penned notes into his log, I said, "Marisela looks like a prostitute."

"No, more likely she's just growing up too fast. Her mother certainly wasn't swayed by us. I hope I didn't push too hard this time. We'll come back."

He was my boss, but one to whom I could talk with liberty. I lobbed in what bothered me about the visit. "I don't know, Mr. Scanlan. I mean, honestly, can we offer anything better than what she's doing? She's already wearing a little gang tattoo."

"Not really, Arturo. Not at this point. We can work on it, but you know the district is cutting my hours. I'll have to work three schools instead of one next year. We can't tell people they can break the law, but we don't want to make a situation worse, either."

Scanlan turned his ignition and quietly rotated his new steering column. I looked across the street at the university apartments and wondered if the blond girls jumping out of their convertibles ever talked to Marisela. We came back a month later, but a different family answered the door, and then other kids took our attention.

A Tiny Triumph

The second visit that day took us out to Vermont Avenue. We stopped for *pupusas*, a Salvadoran tortilla treat with grease, cheese, meat, spices, and a vinegary lettuce topping. On the table was a bottle labeled "MSG" in big letters. It made them tastier. We left the car and walked down to the address. A Mayan mother from Guatemala was in the small front yard clipping plants.

"Si señores. Que les ofresco?" she said as we approached. "What can I offer you?"

"Buenos dias, señora. We work for Adams Junior High School. We've come to talk to you about your daughter."

She took two firm steps with the shears and started in. *"Miren, señores,"* she said. "Look, sirs. I have a big problem with this girl. She won't go to school. Now she wants to dress and talk like a cholita.* I'm afraid she's going to start running away. I can't lock her up. Come inside and talk to her."

Tiny had the same Mayan features as her mother: a petite, oval face and dark, angular features. Unlike our earlier visit, there was energy here. The parent and daughter were animated, and Tiny, who was in seventh grade and just starting the ditching game, appeared excited about our visit. In the house, I asked her about the missing days.

---

* The feminine form of *cholo* or *cholito, cholita* refers to a female gang member.

31

"Its boring, and there's too much problems. The teachers, they don't want to help you." Forty children crowded into classrooms at her school, so I could believe she felt unattended. If that was the problem, the adults in this room might be able to provide a remedy.

The mother said she would personally deliver Tiny to school the next day, and I offered to talk to all her teachers and work out a way to catch up. We made quite a show of seriousness, including getting a commitment from the mother, who worked cleaning houses, that she would follow Tiny from class to class if she didn't start showing up. I was going to check with Tiny's teachers every day to see if this was needed. Tiny made the obligatory protest proper to any self-respecting teenager, but it was obvious she was enjoying the attention.

So we talked tough, surrounded Tiny with both threats and promises of support. The next day, she was in the attendance office, I had her class schedule with me, and we started the day together. I had learned something in the previous months, however. This time around, it would be no one man show. Clint Eastwood was right: We should know our limitations.

I used the school phone and stationery to contact churches and colleges. I asked if they had groups that took an interest in troubled kids. Some of them did. Within two weeks, Emily, a sophomore from USC, and Leticia and Monica, two students at East L.A. City College, had volunteered to help Tiny through the school year.

Leticia and Monica tutored her during the day. The assistant principal agreed that Tiny could be pulled from class and instead study with the volunteers in the cafeteria. Not only were Leticia and Monica excellent tutors, but as successful young Latinas, they inspired Tiny toward a larger vision of her possibilities.

Emily, a descendent of Greek immigrants and a popular and ambitious sorority member at a prestigious university, had a similar effect on Tiny. Emily didn't tutor. Instead, she made home visits, took Tiny to coffee, and took her to school with her. Even though Tiny lived 30 yards from USC, the university had remained invisible to her up to now. Emily changed that. Tiny sat in college chairs, ate in the college cafeteria, and lost herself in the bookstore among the scurrying students complaining about the price of books. It all appeared grand, difficult, and exciting to her, but at least college was real now and a possible future to dream about.

In all, it took nine months, a mother who was willing to miss work on occasion, six cooperative teachers, a flexible school administrator, two tutors, one mentor, and my persistence to make the transformation stick. *Poco a poquito*—little by little— it finally did.

* * * * *

To bend a tree straight, you tether it to a post stronger than the tree itself. Eventually, the rope and the post will be absorbed by the tree, which will grow itself around them. It takes years.

A Puppet Story

Puppet claimed the local Primera Flats gang but met a boy from Diamond Street, so she spent a lot of time downtown, sleeping in cars, in parks, in different people's basements, on their floors, and sometimes on the roof of the Mayflower Hotel, where Diamond Street *veteranos*—older gang members—often spent the night.

Puppet's stepfather had finally convinced her mother of the wisdom in sending Puppet to stay with relatives in El Salvador. He made tamales at night and sold them to local restaurants and on the street while Puppet's mother sold curios from a small cart near McArthur Park. When Puppet told her friends that her stepfather was going to force her to go to El Salvador, they told her, "Just tell a teacher that he touches you and tries to make sex with you at night."

She did. The prosecutor told him that if he pleaded guilty, he would get three months, go to counseling for a year, and be allowed back home in maybe two years. If he fought it, his court-appointed attorney told him, it would be his word against hers, and such cases were difficult to win. If he lost, he could expect several years in prison.

So the tamale vendor pleaded no contest. As long as he stayed away from the house, the other children wouldn't have to go to a foster home, which would have killed their mother. It pained him to say he was sorry for something he had not done. He mostly kept quiet in group therapy, did what the social workers told him, and sold his tamales to help with the rent. In the meantime, Puppet did as she pleased, wandering at will and hanging out with her Diamond Street Gang boyfriend.

On one particular Sunday afternoon, Puppet put on makeup—a thick white base and eyeliner to her ears—plucked her eyebrows to a thin line, and applied a heavy rouge and black lipstick. She took the bus to Maple Street and went to the Mansion—the abandoned house where the gang kids hung out—to kick around until the other boys and girls arrived.

That evening, Big Sleepy,* an older gang member who had considerable artistic talent and had done a mural for the meat man, had a hit of acid, going a little frantic when his tiny white papers blew out over the sidewalk. Popeye, Droopy, and Silent started hitting the paint rag. Goofy, whom no one had ever seen sober, had been sniffing glue most of the day, including between periods at school. He was sharing with Shadow. Sharky had a sherm stick, a cigarette dipped in PCP, which he was enjoying with Creeper.

Shotgun, an obese chola always in black jeans and black sweat top and always looking for a fight, was on the steps taking a hit of acid. Little Joe was drunk, and Mike, who lived in an abandoned car and everyone knew was crazy, grabbed a rag and breathed in deeply, shaking for a few seconds, then smiled.

Little Joe, who once told me his ambition in life was "to have enough money so I can get a cute white boy to drive my limousine in case my ho gets tight," grabbed Shotgun—who, even stoned, was mean—and went downstairs where Puppet was laying on the couch, tanked on paint and acid. They got Dreamer and said, "Let's put Puppet on the train, she's wasted." He knew that Puppet thought Dreamer was cute, and maybe that would make it easier.

During the fire that had created this abandoned house, the living room floor had fallen into the basement, and several feet of front wall had also disappeared. Now a charred sofa, some

---

*   When two gang members share the same placa, one commonly adds "Little" or "Big" to his moniker, signifying which is the younger or older cholo.

chairs and a card table, blankets and rags, bottles, cans, and butts were scattered across a sunken concrete floor. At night, the moon, lights from passing cars, and a street lamp created shadowy gray figures of gang members, with firefly points coming from their cigarettes. Art Laboe was on KRLA radio playing oldies and dedications. Everyone listening could hear that some *flaca* † wanted someone named Bobby to know that "I'll be yours forever."

Dreamer stood over Puppet and dropped his black, pressed khakis. Little Joe let the others know he was next. That was Sunday night.‡

---

† Literally, "skinny." *Flaca* or *flaco* is a common Spanish nickname.

‡ Although I wasn't there, from what I saw the next morning, I believe this story, as told to me by the gang members, to be true.

PART TWO

GATHERING THE
CHILDREN OF THE GANG

Condemned Places

Puppet should have been in high school by now. She was 16, and this made her technically ineligible for junior high school. As soon as someone caught up with her, I was sure school officials would tell her this.

With Mr. Scanlan, I contacted both her mother and her stepfather. Officially, he couldn't help us until the court let him back in the home. In the interim, Puppet's mother had lost the little control she had over her. I understood that much from the visits.

Looking over her records, and making a couple of phone calls to her elementary schools, I understood a bit more. Everywhere, I heard the same comments: She was a bright girl but impulsive, confrontational, and hyperactive. She tended to say things that teachers didn't enjoy hearing. In junior high, this had finally resulted in two "opportunity transfers" (OTs), the euphemism for being expelled from one school and sent to another within the L.A. Unified School District.

When she never showed up for her first OT, she drew a second and ended up at Adams. After several months, her total attendance added up to 17 complete days, none of them recent. I had noticed Puppet only once on the playground, hanging around the boys from Clanton and Primera Flats. She was tiny—could have passed for a 12- or 13-year-old in heavy makeup.

The best bet would be that she partied at the Mansion along with the other gang kids. Where else would she be? The options in this neighborhood were limited. I decided I finally had the comfort with the area and with enough of the kids for me to pay a visit.

Tiny had continued to do well, and although she kept her old friends, she had now made new and different ones. In fact, she had taken the initiative to begin a volleyball team at the local recreation center and was recruiting adults to drive them around. She had become my ally, partially because she liked me and partially because, like all kids, she wanted the best for her friends. When I asked her about Puppet, Tiny said, yes, she knew her and she did hang out at the Mansion. Tiny immediately volunteered to help me find her.

On Monday morning—the day after the party at the Mansion—Tiny checked in with me before school, as had become our routine. There was little urgency to this anymore, but it provided a minute to be acknowledged, wished a good day, asked about homework, and such. I asked her if we could visit the Mansion today after lunch. She agreed to take me. I had already cleared it with Mr. Scanlan and the assistant principal.

Walking back across the school yard, I saw two boys fighting outside the truancy office. I tried to separate them, but one of the combatants beaned me with a trash can when I grabbed his adversary. The school administrator, Mrs. Lewis, a large, grandmotherly woman, had no trouble settling things down. Juan, our custodian, pulled me back into the office and took the ice tray out of the miniature fridge. He snapped the cubes out with a rap on the edge of my desk, poured them into a paper towel, and handed me the bundle to put against my head.

With the small bump on my cap still thumping, I waited for Tiny to get to her fifth-period class, check out, and meet me for a tour of the Clanton–Primera Flats Mansion. She shared little of my apprehension. In fact, she thought it was a good idea to go right to where everyone would be and straighten them out. Give them a good talking to. Like most kids, she ignored that the alchemy of her newfound success took time and was generated from the efforts of no small number of adults. As Tiny saw it, she had simply seen the light, and her friends were stupid and stubborn for not doing likewise.

We walked up Figueroa a few blocks, twisting our way through a crowd of Vietnamese and Latina ladies who were Ping-Ponging between a row of sewing shops and the lunch truck. The Vietnamese women were eating something with a hot pungency I didn't recognize. We turned down 13th toward Maple.

"This is where it is, in that house. That's the Mansion."

The house had once risen handsomely, two stories with a little attic on top. It had caught fire and now stood gutted and charred, with the rear kitchen and part of the living room exposed. Burnt furniture sat on the yellowed grass, surrounded by paint cans, beer cans, shoes, bottles, bike parts, and a TV. In the middle of the lawn rested an orange couch with a very sleepy boy on it. We came up over him and his head popped up. His eyes were watery, and the whole lower half of his face was covered in silver paint. I recognized him.

"Silent," Tiny said, "Mr. Hernandez is here to talk to you."

"Who?"

"The counselor. Don't act stupid."

He wanted to get pissed off, but a roulette wheel took off in his head when he tried to sit up. "I think we should look in the Mansion," I whispered in Tiny's ear. I didn't know if Silent remembered my visit to his apartment, but it didn't matter in his current condition.

"Homeboys had a party last night," Silent managed to puff out at us. I stood there with Tiny and watched Silent fall back asleep. At least I knew where he stayed now, and for today that might be enough.

We left Silent on the couch and walked around the back of the house. Little Joe—who had a sumo figure with a round, shaved head, so that he was all circles, like a snowman—was leaning on the door frame. *"Wátchale,"** he said sarcastically. "Tiny brought a narc."

---

* 　Watch out.

"That's Little Joe," she told me.

I put out my hand to him. "It looks like you guys had a *fiestecita** last night."

"Whasup, Homey," he said, waving off my hand. "You come to close down our *cantón?*† You missed out, Homeboy. We put Puppet on the train last night."

We looked inside. Puppet was asleep in a huddle with two boys on the floor. A short boy walked in from outside. With each step, Sharky's knees almost touched the ground before bouncing back up in a jerky, stylized walk that reminded me of a marionette. He came in, carrying what looked like a car fender on his shoulder, and proclaimed, "Insane, no brain!" Then he turned to Popeye, who was on the stairs, and said, "How you like this poem: 'When I was from Flats, I was bad. Now I'm from Clanton, I'm *matón.'* ‡ It's bad, huh Homie?" He turned to me. "You work with Mrs. Lewis?"

"You go to Adams?"

"Yeah, Homeboy. I'm taking a vacation today, me and Popeye."

"Tell your Uncle Popeye what you want, Homes," Popeye said to me.

"Tell me who you're hiding in those pants." Every gang kid had his or her own call to distinction. For Popeye, it was all about pants, and his had true '40s Pachuco flair—pants that started tight at the ankles, billowed wide as the sails, and pulled tight again near his chest. A head and huge pants is what you saw when you saw Popeye.

"Ooo, shit," Smiley said. "Homeboy's baggin' on your pants."

"How many people can you fit on that forehead?" he came back with a shot at my five-finger top.

A diminutive African American girl in cornrows came in. "You tell that big old white man I see you with to stay out of my

---

*   A little party.

†   Home.

‡   A killer.

business, or I'll shoot him with a bullet." The kitchen was getting crowded.

"I'll tell him when I get back," I said. "What's your name?"

"You don't need nobody's name. You here for the ditching party or what?"

"So is everyone going back to class? Lunch is over. Or do I have to arrest everybody?" It was a bluff, meant to reestablish my authority among them.

Everyone started opining and complaining at the same time—"You can't arrest nobody," "*Chale,** take out the cuffs, Homes"—and all kinds of other talk. Sharky came up to me and faked a punch, slapping his fist into his palm in front of my face. It made a good, swift "whack." "I'll have to knock you out, Homes."

Tiny didn't like the banter. "He only came to talk to Silent and Puppet."

"*Chale,*"† Droopy said to me. He had a lisp that made it come out sounding like "Shale." "You should have come last night." Like Silent, out front on the couch, Droopy and Popeye both had silver mouths from sniffing paint and were giddy still, with constant grins. Their bodies swayed, like they were picking up slow grounders, as they talked.

"Tiny," I said, "you know Puppet. Why don't you go get her and have her come back with us?"

"You have to go. She's hardheaded."

The little girl in cornrows asked, "What you want with her?"

I had expected them to ask this, and I decided to lie a little so this meeting we were having might turn into some kind of beginning. "I might have jobs for kids."

"Why don't you give me a job?" Popeye asked.

" 'Cause they don't got jobs sniffing paint," Little Joe informed him.

"Maybe they got a job being fat and stupid," Popeye shot back.

---

* In this context, *chale* means "Come on."

† In this context, *chale* means "No way."

"Anyway," I cut in, "tell Puppet to come see me when she wakes up. Anyone else who wants to talk about a job, just come to my office. It doesn't matter if you're ditching."

When I got back outside with Tiny, she questioned my improvisation. "Are you really going to get jobs, or you were just messing around?"

"I'm going to try. Maybe we could form, like, a club, have some meetings."

"That would be good, but you need to tell all the homeboys when. I can tell Smiley and Droopy at school."

"Why don't you just ask the ones that you think are the most serious, and you guys will be the leaders. That way we can think about what we're doing." This was a stall for time, but it appealed to her, and she said she would think about it and come see me later.

* * * * *

A friend traveled to Yugoslavia during the war and told me that people had become monsters, that neighbors maimed each others' children. She returned recently and could not believe that people were just people again. In fear, most people degenerate quickly; in hope, they revive just as miraculously. After the school notified the police, the city razed the Mansion, and many of the kids who used to go there became involved in club activities. Most could not remember abusing each other as they once had in that place.

How I Almost Wiped Out
the Whole Gang

I had long been aware that many people—recreation leaders, activists, pastors—sponsored clubs of some sort or another for gang-involved kids. The predicament these youths presented easily engendered an urge to gather them up.

Nearly all gangs have a park in their neighborhoods that they claim as their own and where they spend most of their time. This creates dilemmas for park directors who do not like the intimidating fact of their presence, but the law allows access to anyone, and that includes groups of troubled teenagers. The Clanton and Primera Flats gangs shared a park, and after the Mansion was razed, this became the only large, public space they could inhabit. Of course, the park did not provide the kind of cover they had at the old house—a marked improvement of the situation.

As far as starting a club, the park made it easy to round up gang kids. I would just mention to either Tiny, Smiley, Popeye, Droopy, or Sharky that we were having a meeting or event, and they would pass the word to whoever happened to be hanging around the park. Like most teenagers, gang members were often bored and looking for something different to do.

Still, this wasn't quite the same as starting a bowling league or youth group. These kids were in trouble, and I wanted to do more than just keep them busy for a few hours a week. I met

often with their parents and teachers and, like them, I worried
and wondered about what to do next that would make enough
of a difference.

Club leaders gathered in my office at Adams during lunch
and talked about things like camping trips, car washes, club
jackets, rules of conduct, and job hunting for the older members—basic youth group stuff. But I didn't fool myself that this
was going to be just another after-school scout troop. I needed
help. I needed other adults to create ideas, share responsibility,
and keep our spirits in good health. It was all about teamwork—
no crazy heroics, just good, well-rehearsed teamwork.

I called the local junior college and made appointments to
speak to classes in psychology, Chicano studies, and crimi-
nology about volunteers. People taking these classes would
have an interest in troubled kids, especially those in gangs, and
might want to help. And they did, of course. Chico, a slight man
in his late 20s who walked with a limp and cane, volunteered to
tutor after school and supervise outings. Others offered to
drive, mentor, chaperone, conduct bake sales, and sew insignias
on jackets.

One man began to help regularly: Mark Fretland—six-foot-
five, full beard—a quiet, religious man in his 20s from the
Midwest who decided to take equal leadership with me. Soon,
we were talking each other into making a greater commitment
to this neighborhood. Mark and I rented one of the sewing
factories on 41st and Main and moved into its long concrete
space. We made a shower by attaching hoses to a hot water pipe
that ran through our building to the bathroom next door. After
taking a shower, we would empty the gray water by sliding our
plastic tub out to the sidewalk. The place was cheap and loud but
perfect for meetings and overnights. A band that called itself
"Coco's Troprock" rehearsed next door, and I occasionally
jammed with them.

Mark worked downtown, and on the way home he used to
pick up bags of day-old cinnamon rolls from Grand Central
Market on the bus. We shared these with the kids who came for

meetings. Lots of days, all we ate were cinnamon rolls, but they were good.

Besides the cholos we were organizing, we also started a different club. The landlord of the huge Norwood tenements had given tenants permission to use the basement as a meeting area. We knew that immigrant families were crammed into those apartments, and we wanted to become part of prevention efforts as well as to work with gang members. Since the landlord offered the space, we offered to provide a club for the teens in the building. Every night, one of us would meet with the kids from the Norwood Street tenements and teach them how to write essays. I knew they hated to do this is school, but it was fun in the basement. You had to be 12 years old to come down and join us. We would pick a topic, talk about it, write an opinion or story, and then have punch and cookies. We had a full basement every night.

Of course, for both the gang members from the junior high and the kids from the Norwood tenements, the promise of fun and field trips provided most of the motivation to participate. Our big event, promised to both groups—and one we had been talking about for months—involved a three-day camping trip in the nearby San Gabriel Mountains and the Angeles National Forest. The gang members, the Norwood kids, and the youth from St. Vincent's Acción Catolica youth group were all invited.* We didn't have the time to take each group on their own weekend, and we hoped, by mixing the kids, there would be less chance of irresponsible behavior on the part of a few of the gang members.

---

*   If you are only familiar with youth groups in the United States, going to an Acción Catolica [Catholic Action] meeting will give you a quick lesson on what *youth* means in different cultures. Acción Catolica is a youth movement throughout the Spanish-speaking world. Unlike American-style youth groups, Acción Catolica groups are autonomous, with a priest serving only as a mentor. Here are 14- to 25-year-olds intermingling and discussing sending money to aid Salvadoran guerrillas, planning dances at local discos, and scheduling speakers for their next seminars.

The only objections came from mothers concerning their daughters. Patricia Avila, a very traditional, very Mexican, very articulate friend of mine, volunteered to chaperone. She convinced uneasy parents there would be no chance for monkey business under her watch.

Maria Elena, one of the kids, got her father to lend us his pickup. Dario, another kid, brought his Galaxy 500; still another kid, Yogi, brought his van; and I brought the 1973 brown Chevy Econoline I had just purchased for $800. Mark and Patricia went for the kids from the Norwood apartments. Dario picked up the Acción Catolica group at St. Vincent's.

Yogi and I went to get the Primera Flats and Clanton boys at the park. On the way, we picked up Creeper, Popeye, Smiley, and Droopy. Popeye had a suitcase with a blanket and food, Smiley took a book bag from his sister that he stuffed with boiled eggs and a jacket, and Droopy had a sleeping bag and a poncho. It was a three-day hike, and it was going to get cold. Creeper, one of only three African Americans in the gang, brought his two cousins visiting from Louisiana. They were sent to keep an eye on him; one of them was a 14-year-old girl who was thin-boned and wore a large, metal back brace. Her mother was not overprotective of her, which I thought was cool.

At the park, there were kids I didn't know but who said they wanted to go. After a fast lecture on no guns, drugs, rags, paint, glue, or markers, I said anyone could go, but we had to go by their homes and get permission. That thinned the numbers immediately.

Goofy said it would be no problem. We drove to his little square house, which was connected to others in a barrack-like row. We entered and went to the bedroom, where his mother was in front of a vanity with lots of bright bulbs. She was in a black dancing dress and was putting on lipstick. I think she worked in a bar. He just walked behind her and said in his subdued voice, "Mom, I'm going to the mountains with Art."

"When will you be back?"

"Monday."

Even though she knew me, she still looked intimidated—afraid to say no or to question me. Her eyes went back and forth between Goofy and me, the ways dogs look when they're afraid to cross traffic. It was the look she had when Mr. Scanlan and I brought Goofy in for an assessment and she just sat there with all the psychologists, not saying a word the whole meeting, just signing things and nodding.

Goofy went into the kitchen and came out with a loaf of bread and some peanut butter. He grabbed a blanket off his bed, and we went back out to the van.

We met up at St. Vincent's, and Father Sharp blessed the cars. It was a late start, and it was dark when we arrived at the trail. We walked by flashlight and slept the first night in a clearing about a mile from the cars.

Popeye talked about his father as we put a fire together to warm us and to burn some marshmallows before slipping into our bags and covers. "Everyone thinks my *jefecito*[*] is crazy, but I understand him. Everyone treats him like he's stupid."

"Is something wrong with him?" I asked. I had met his father: He was old and slow, with short white hair. He had worked hard his whole life, and now his body was like a gnawed-up dog chew.

"He fell and hit his head, and now my mother wants to make an excuse to put him in a home. 'I'll go get him out,' I told her."

I would remember this conversation a few days later. One of the reasons Mark and I had rented the warehouse space was so the kids could do sleepovers. It was a treat for them. A week after our camping trip, Popeye asked if he could spend the night. His eyes and his voice betrayed his fear—an emotion this 15-year-old usually hid well—and I said yes. But that evening I changed my mind. I had just broken up with my girlfriend and wasn't feeling like company. I made up some excuse and told him he couldn't come over.

---

[*] *Jefecito* is the diminutive form of *jefe*—literally, a chief or leader. The diminutive and its feminine form, *jefecita,* are often used to refer to one's father or mother as head of the family.

"How come you don't want me at your pad?" he asked with a bag full of his stuff over his shoulder.

"I just can't. Next week for sure."

But a few days later, Popeye's father left for a nursing home. Popeye got drunk and drove the family car straight through Trinity Park on a Saturday afternoon, bowling through picnics, the Ping Pong tables, a small soccer game, and two basketball games. No one died, fortunately, but children were injured, and many people could have been killed. Popeye was sent to prison until he turned 25—the maximum for a minor. It would have been longer if he had killed anyone. I've had guilt about this for years.

But no one responded to Popeye's problem as he talked about his father by the campfire. Most of the campers had already tucked themselves away, and the sleepless few talked in snippets while hunched over the fire.

That night, the cold made everyone want to pee. They had to get out of their blankets or bags to do it, which made them colder, so then they had to pee again when they got back in. In the morning, Joker showed the boys how he kept a Coke bottle in his bag so he didn't need to get out. Happy said it was the worst night of his life.

At breakfast, we pulled our *pan de dulce** from the bottoms of our packs, where they had flattened out. We ended up dipping the sweetbreads in a mixture of Ovaltine and river water and ate while packing up.

We started toward Mount Wilson, about seven miles upstream. Silent insisted on leading the group, but he mistook thin avenues in the brush for actual trails and kept getting us stuck on hillsides and dead ends. He was hiking in tennis shoes, which made him slip on the wet rocks whenever we crossed the river. But no one laughed.

Because they are cheap and available, paints, adhesives, and solvents are the drug of choice among poor teenagers the world over. Many of our gang-involved boys could not get through a

---

*   Mexican sweetbreads.

day without the high from a can of spray paint. Knowing this, I checked them as thoroughly as I could without being too invasive. Still, we didn't leave the problem back in the city.

Toward noon, we found some pools and a waterfall and took a sandwich and swim break. Immediately, several in the group warned us that our two clowns, Popeye and Droopy, could not be found. Sometime between breakfast and lunch, the two of them had fallen to the back of the group and then disappeared without notice.

Luis, an older boy from Acción Catolica, volunteered to backtrack and find them. I decided we couldn't keep hiking until they reappeared; if it took longer than two hours, we would all have to go back and find a park ranger.

No need. About two hours later, Luis returned with them literally in tow—he had them on a tether, silver-faced and laughing boisterously, their feet slipping from under them as they stumbled into camp.

Popeye had a knack for the ridiculous. On an earlier field trip, he had almost gotten himself and my brother, who was chaperoning, kicked out of Disneyland when Popeye stopped his car in Autotopia and created a funride traffic jam. He got out of his car and just sat on the hood in his gigantic baggy pants, with his sideways grin and droopy eyes, telling people, "Uncle Popeye wants everyone to slow down and have fun."

But as funny as Popeye and Droopy now appeared, the pathos of the situation wasn't lost on anyone. Maybe that kept the others, if they had planned on getting stoned this way, from actually carrying it out.

Luis stayed with Popeye and Droopy for the next leg of the hike. The trail elevated at this point and sometimes narrowed to a couple of feet along the side of the mountain. The paint had wrecked their coordination, and a slip here could send them 40 feet into the river below.

Patricia watched the girls, especially her little sister, as romance was inevitable. The girls found the gang boys cute, but living with them for three days was taking some of their shine off.

We eventually hiked to a place where snow appeared in patches all around us. The river went underground at that point, and a steep switchback trail led up to Mt. Wilson. From there, our campers could choose to hike as far up the mountain as they wanted, or they could hang out at the base, take a break, and explore the locale.

I started out with Patricia, Freddy, Silent, Maria, and a restored Droopy to try and make it to the summit. About halfway up, I tired of looking at the trail eight inches from my face, and wimped out. I left with a slight apprehension, because I could tell that Maria and Droopy had a little romance brewing, but I trusted Pat to keep an eye on the situation. We all met back at the camp around three o'clock for a late lunch of hard boiled eggs, peanut butter sandwiches, and tortillas with cheese and chili.

The delay waiting for Popeye and Dopey had thrown off my calculations. Our plans were approximate to start with and not based on the kind of research about temperature, weather, and daylight that real outdoorsmen or -women take into consideration. My mountain experience consisted of a few day hikes and a couple of overnighters in this same forest.

Around six o'clock, we began hiking back to a clearing about 40 minutes downstream, but the evening set fast and the sun vanished on us. It got a lot colder. The forest began to lose color, and the trees absorbed the gray of the rocks. For some unexplained reason, no one could find the flashlights. I had never been hiking on a moonless night. In the city, there's always some light—you can always see something. I put my hand right at my nose, and it wasn't there.

It began to rain. I had thought it might, but I didn't think a light rain would be dangerous. From under the huge trees, it would look pretty. I'd never really been camping outside of these local hills, where teenagers went to make out in the evenings. It was impossible to me that they could be dangerous.

The group compressed. All light was gone, and you could only tell who was around by voice.

"If I die, Homes, my mom's gonna sue your ass."

"Where are you? Is everyone okay?"

Everyone started yelling. From the back, they were saying, "The water's going up too much."

I'd also never been hiking during a storm. A stream rises just like water in a tub. The trail was gone, and the stream, which had been seven feet away, spread across the canyon floor and then moved up to our knees. Everyone was staying against the smooth sides of the canyon.

"*Pendejo,** I said to myself, "this is how that shit you read about in the papers happens: 'Idiot counselor trapped in canyon with teens and no flashlight. All drown.' " We were only two miles above Arcadia, which meant our bodies would wash up tomorrow morning at the Santa Anita Fashion Mall or the racetrack.

Kids were now holding on tightly to shrubbery. "Where are we going?" people were shouting. But the sound of the water had grown as loud as our voices. The girl with the back brace tried not to cry. No one wanted to move anymore. The stream had become a river that pulled against our legs. No one could see the faces next to them.

"I'm climbing up to see what's here," said Casper, who sounded like he was in front. He disappeared for two or three minutes. Everyone got quiet. Then we heard him shout down, "There's a little patch up here we can fit into I think. Tell everyone to come up. I'll help them."

"Start going up," Mark told those in front. "Just follow the wall."

"The packs are too heavy," someone complained

"Throw them in the water," someone else answered.

"That's my shit. I need it."

"You wanna drown with it, stupid?"

People went up slowly, following the voices in front of and above them. Patricia and two of the boys inserted themselves

---

* *Pendejo* is a term used primarily in Mexico and indicates that one is a fool or idiot of elevated proportions.

like spikes up the side of the hill to buttress and guide those crawling up. At the back of the procession waited Droopy, the girl with the brace, and me.

"I'll take the little *chavala,*"* Droopy offered. "Just put her on my back." He was thin but hard, with long arms that felt like well-inflated tires. I had the girl in a lock, with one arm tight around her waist, trying not to push the brace into her skin. I could tell it hurt. I tilted her onto Droopy's back, and she did a monkey wrap around him with her legs and arms. Droopy leaned into the hill, looking for edges to lock his long fingers into. I could hear the slow alternation of a hand, followed by another hand, then followed by a foot, then the other foot, and then his fingers again, looking for something jagged and solid to curl around.

The laughing, blaming, and cursing didn't go on very long in the rain. We huddled and waited. We spent a very long time in the dark. No one slept that night, and no one had food to eat the next morning.

With the first bluish light, we became aware that we had climbed up to a large campground and could have moved a few yards to some shelter. But the temperature dropped right before sunrise, so we all got up and began moving—sloshing for the most part—back up the hill to our cars.

Mark and I got blamed for all of the suffering. But the kids talked about that trip for months—and now years. It was complained about rather fondly. I counted the trip a success.

In our ultimate aim, however, we were failing.

The club kept the kids busy, the trips were fun, and some of the tutoring and badgering had helped a bit. But we were disconnected from the most important parts of the day and from the real tasks of growing up. Our work had nothing to do with school and family and the real process, day in and day out, of learning how to become an adult. I still could not get the gang members to succeed in, or even attend, school. I had no power against their addictions, and I could not help their parents keep

---

*   *Chavala* is slang for *girl.*

them home at night. Yet, I saw that their parents, teachers, and probation officers were all well-intentioned and working as hard as they could to help these kids.

What I had learned, several times over now, was that success depended on gathering several different kinds of adults together and surrounding the gang members throughout the day with help. Organizing such an effort took time, and in the end I could only reach a small number of children. Yet, nearly all the gang members responded positively to offers of help. It became obvious that gathering the gang members in one place all day would be much more efficient than trying to reach them as they scattered throughout this large school and crazy neighborhood.

Everything But the Money

In the 10th grade, I began giving clarinet lessons, my first real job. Mrs. Macias paid me $4 to teach her daughter, and I could stay for dinner as well. I don't know if her intention favored music or the idea that, as a church boy, I would be a good influence on Kathy. Either way, I took the music end of it very seriously. All through high school, I developed private students.

I paid for my first year of college by continuing private lessons and working as a singing monkey for a delivery service called Gorilla Gram. I'd show up on a yellow moped with a banjo and a tap-dancing brunette, and the two of us would musically deliver a message. The gig vacuumed its share of dignity, but I have always preferred independent kinds of employment.

My second year of college, I met another guitarist, Mark Olvera, and we got jobs at El Azteca in San Gabriel, offering table-to-table romantic serenades to diners. Mark also gave private lessons, so we teamed up and opened our own music school. We had no idea how much time a new business took. We had sleeping bags in the closet, because we seldom left before midnight and had clients first thing in the morning. After a year, we decided to close the business as it would keep us from ever finishing college. But it gave me experience in running a small operation, working with employees, and developing a teaching program. When the conservatory closed, I applied for the job at Adams.

I liked working with Mr. Scanlan. Being on the road with him proved interesting, and he gave me the freedom to be his partner and not just a translator. Besides helping the truant officer, half of my salary involved coordinating a program between USC and our junior high school. The university set guidelines for how its students should be used, and my job was to follow them and so place these volunteers with classrooms throughout the school. I, however, funneled all the university volunteers into situations where they worked with gang members. This did not meet the program's intentions. USC rightfully asked that I be replaced with someone who didn't have such an overt agenda and such a hard head when it came to just doing what I had been asked.

The administration at Adams should have canned me, but they were a wise, confident bunch; and if not for one of the assistant principals, Marilyn Nuerenberg, I would have left the neighborhood, and nothing more would have occurred.

Mrs. Nuerenberg replaced me in the position, as USC had requested; but instead of firing me, she took some money from somewhere in the budget and gave me a desk, a phone, 15 paid hours a week, and the following directions: "Half the day, keep working with Mr. Scanlan. But you have the other half to do something for the gang members at Adams. Be creative." That was it. She was a smart lady and good manager. She knew what to do with someone like me.

So with time to think, and the dilemma of what to do with the gang members I had gathered, an idea began to percolate. For all of their nettlesome behavior, and in part because of it, I loved and enjoyed Smiley, Droopy, Popeye, Happy, and all these other characters. Instead of chasing gang kids around and trying to force them into classrooms in which they failed, couldn't we start a place from scratch that developed with their needs in mind and their success at heart? I approached Mr. Siskel, the other assistant principal, with the idea. I suspect a lesser person would have patronized this 22-year-old assistant to the truancy counselor. Instead, Mr. Siskel encouraged me. "Look into it," he said, "and keep us informed."

In the following weeks, my principal, Dr. Ikeda; Mrs. Nuerenberg; Mr. Siskel; and Mr. Scanlan all sat with me at various times or stood with me in the lunch yard while I was on supervision. They helped detail what such a place would be like. It would have a master teacher, but volunteers and paid aides would reduce the adult-student ratio to one adult per five students. Every kid would get personal attention. We would also involve probation officers, a family therapist, and liaisons with as many community resource providers as possible. The new school would provide field trips and ceremonies and concentrate on positive experiences. Parents would be our partners.

Space proved the limitation. Overcrowded, Adams had several student tracks that ran year-round. Even stair wells and broom closets were used for instruction. The only solution, in my view, would be for the school district to purchase a large, industrial building, on the corner of the PE yard, that had been put up for sale. I made telephone calls to everyone in town and circulated a petition among police officers, local ministers, probation directors, and business people asking the school board to consider purchasing the building. Then I arranged a meeting with Rita Walters, our Board of Education member, and Sid Thompson, our regional supervisor.

Mrs. Walters and Mr. Thompson liked the idea and took it to the Board of Education as a request. But it all came down to money. The building owner wanted much more than the district could pay. Without a space, the idea ran aground—except by now I had told the gang kids, in my own one-step-ahead optimism, that the idea was a sure thing. They would have their own place. I had been talking it up for weeks.

There was no way to just let this go.

If you call enough people, someone out there has an answer. Out of curiosity, and with suspicion that there might be an avenue here, I called departments throughout the city and then the state until I found the person in charge of legitimizing private schools. I asked him what it took to open a private school in California.

Nothing. No requirements.

As long as the building met safety codes, and the school director forwarded a list of who attended and what courses they were taking, anyone could open a school. The teachers did not have to possess any particular set of credentials. Even a former employee of Gorilla Gram could establish one.

The only immediate impediment to taking the idea from Adams and going private was, of course, the one thing that wasn't available, and seldom is.

Money.

What Sugar Ray Would Do

The news from our small television provided background noise while Mark and I tore open the boil-in-bag rice. We talked about the gang kids, as we always did at dinner. Our efforts to help them were stalled, and we both knew it. For the time being, Mark had decided to concentrate on the Norwood tenement project, and I really didn't know where to go with the school idea.

We stopped talking and listened to the television for a minute.

Mark heard the engine first. Then I tuned in. Like dogs, our ears flipped toward the direction of the door.

"That sounds like your van," Mark said, standing up.

"Hey," we both barked. We ran toward the door.

Sure enough, the brown Econoline, with the new stereo that Yogi and Casper had put in for free, was turning the corner.

"Didn't you have a kill switch?" a neighbor asked.

"Yeah," I said sheepishly. "They must have found it." But I was lying. This was one of the few times I hadn't turned it on. I had thought about doing it—it would have only taken a few more seconds—but I was hungry.

As I was about to learn, a lot of things can happen riding the bus.

I often visited and spent the night with my parents in Highland Park. Without the Econoline, this meant an early morning bus ride back to the truancy office. I got on at the beginning of the line, but within a mile there were people standing. There was no chivalry; young men like myself sat comfortably while old ladies took flight in the aisles every time the bus came to a stop. They were too weak to hold onto the rails, and only the other bodies, thickly packed, kept them in place.

When I took an evening bus back to Highland Park, we had to pick up the people who worked at the Farmer John meat-packing plant. We also picked up the people who worked for the produce wholesalers, the Chinese fish markets, and the live-poultry dealer on Florence. They all smelled quite different coming home than they did in the mornings.

On one such ride, a Vietnamese girl sat next to me. We rode a few more stops, and then an old blind man in a black sailor cap got on. He tried to find a clearing for himself as people did football maneuvers around him to get on or off. The girl stretched out her arm, grabbed the blind man's hand, and pulled him toward her. In one move she got up and pushed him into her seat. It seemed to be a part of her to do this, she did it so naturally.

Her consideration embarrassed me, so I offered her my seat and stood into the crowd. With my arms upstretched to hold onto the overhead handrail, I busied myself by scanning the small ads that formed a row over the windows. Amidst the ads for credit dentists and personal injury lawyers was one from the Campaign for Human Development. Beneath a picture of an open hand against a black background, small white letters offered a telephone number and seed money for community self-help projects.

I immediately remembered something that had been passed on to me about Sugar Ray Robinson, the great boxer whose youth foundation kept a lot of kids busy in this part of town. I had just finished a soccer coaching assignment with the Sugar Ray Robinson Youth Foundation. He gave us balls, a bus, and uniforms. Even though they didn't play soccer, Creeper and Smiley had joined the team for the trips around town to different games. During the next to last game, they had disappeared and come back with shovels and garden tools from somewhere. So, during the last game, I said they had to stay with the team and play. I made the mistake, however, of putting them on defense. This weakened the team and made everyone play too hard, so that one of our players took a spill, breaking one arm and spraining the other.

Taking care of the team medical insurance for the injured player involved going over to the Sugar Ray headquarters. I told one of the supervisors about my disappointment at not being able to open a school for the gang kids.

"Do you know how Sugar Ray would handle this?" he asked. "When Sugar Ray goes to a congressman and asks for funding, he knows the congressman is always going to start up with the ifs: 'If we can talk someone into it. If it fits into the budget.' Sugar Ray stops them before they can get in more than one if. He tells them, 'It's not *if,* it's *how. How* can we get this done? Not *if* we can get it done.' If you stay with the how, you eventually find a way." That advice has never failed me.

On the bus I found a possible how. I borrowed a pen from the man next to me and wrote down the phone number on my forearm. I still had it there when I talked to Sister Natalia later that afternoon.

Catholic Charities operated a small community center called El Santo Niño (the Holy Child) near the junior high school. On Sundays, it functioned as a church when a priest from St. Vincent's would hold services there. The rest of the week, kids came for day care or after-school activities. Sister Natalia Duran directed the center. She was 36 years old, beautiful, and an activist—not that those three have any relation to each other, but they were qualities that defined her at the time. I remember how she used to lay in the driveway of the immigration service to prevent the deportation of Salvadoran refugees. She had vision and nerve.

Sister Natalia gave me a part-time job at the center running after-school groups when I quit my job at Adams to pursue the idea of starting a private school. No one had asked me to leave, but I felt uneasy using a public school job to open a private school, especially when everyone at Adams had been so good to me. So Sister Natalia bought me some time.

When I told her about the ad I had seen on the bus, Sister Natalia directed me to the regional director of Catholic Charities, Sister Georgianna, who was from the same order. Sister Natalia thought that Sister Georgianna would be able to help me with the grant from the Campaign for Human Development and maybe even offer space for the school at El Santo Niño.

I remember two conversations with Sister Georgianna. In one, she told me that it was necessary to have radical nuns who blocked driveways and created social disturbances, but it was also necessary to have nuns within the system who did not overtly attack it and who could go to Washington, D.C., and negotiate deals that might save the same refugees Sister Natalia cared for. That made sense to me. Like working with kids, you need to both push them and also support them. There are always two bookends.

The second conversation occurred on the phone from her hospital bed. She had taken ill soon after I mailed her a copy of my grant proposal. She not only took it with her to the hospital, but Sister Georgianna offered to support the proposal. She let me know that Catholic Charities was not in the school business and that, officially, she could only approve an intensive tutoring project. In spite of that disclaimer, she understood that a tutoring project taking place every day from 9:00 to 3:00 would be, de facto, a school. As much an activist and risk taker as Sister Natalia, she went to the legal limit with me. She would support me, but for one year only. This would provide a start, and then we would see what could be done from there.

She passed on the proposal to a bishop whose job consisted of commending projects to the grant selection committee. The bishop asked her bluntly, "Do you really believe in this project?" She told him yes.

The Campaign for Human Development awarded us a $10,000 grant. It wasn't much money to put a school together, but it was more money than I had ever seen. Besides, my aunt in Mexico had started her first school by holding class under a shade tree on my grandfather's farm.

I did a little math. If I hired a second teacher, and we each made $600 a month, the money would be gone before year's end. If I charged 30 students $20 a month, however, we'd actually have some money left to buy a few things for the classroom. I knew the parents of even the poorest student could come up with $5 a week, and a token payment might even make the school a bit more valuable to everyone.

Sister Georgianna gave me the auditorium at El Santo Niño to use without charge and administered the grant for me. She also put us under the umbrella of Catholic Charities for non-profit status. Frankly, she covered my backside to give these kids at least one year.

I wrote a letter to the state superintendent of private schools. I told him a school was operating by the name of El Santo Niño and that classes were being held at a Catholic Charities site. The superintendent didn't need to know anything about profit or nonprofit status. He just asked two questions: Did the fire marshal okay the site, and where would student files be kept for the next 10 years? I forwarded a certificate for the first question and gave my parents' address for the second.

I had dinner that night at Smiley's house and asked his parents if he could attend the new school. They said yes, and I had my first student. I also asked his sister out on a date, and she said maybe. All in all, it was a very good beginning.

* * * * *

When I was younger, a 19-year-old illegal immigrant from Mexico had been helping the amateur gardeners in my neighborhood. Chemo had recently arrived from an Indian village in Qaxaca. He told me while fertilizing my mother's lawn one day that he had seen a program on television about a place called Argentina. The country had life and opportunity, and the people were good.

Chemo came from a village of 200 people who planted corn with sticks and carried water. He had been to second grade. He disappeared soon after our conversation. The neighbors say he went to Argentina.

Much gets accomplished in this world by people who refuse to consider how impossible a journey might be. In their minds, they have already arrived, and reality just has to catch up.

Books, or Sharky Goes to Prep School

I heard from Miquelito, the custodian at El Santo Niño, about the drive-by that had occurred out front the previous December. He had heard the shots outside, carried the 13-year-old in from the sidewalk, and laid him on the soft cotton snow under the auditorium's large Christmas tree. He could do nothing except hold the young cholito, life falling away through the small bullet holes in the boy's neck.

In that same corner of the auditorium, Miquelito and I now placed a table, two chairs, and on the table a globe with sunken valleys and ridged mountains you could feel with your fingers.

I put away the altar, chairs, and candles, but left the big cross, St. Martin, and the Virgin. I organized 10 folding picnic tables into three rows. The lumber yard on Central Avenue donated a long slab of plywood and several cans of blackboard paint; the owner taught me how to use them to make a durable chalkboard.

The local grocers also pitched in on supplies. "Food for Life" volunteered to give us bread for sandwiches once a week, and Iris, a local food wholesaler, donated gallon cans of peanut butter and jam. Not much variety, but at least we would have sandwich stuff available if students forgot to bring sack lunches from home.

I began looking for a second teacher, someone who could work for $600 dollars a month and have a good time doing it for

one year. I asked Mark if he wanted to take it on, but he had
school to finish and by this time was devoting all his extra
energy to keeping the tenement club at Norwood functioning.
So I put out an offer of employment.

The advertisements on university job boards and local papers elicited plenty of replies. Unfortunately, most of the appli-
cants wanted absolute guarantees of safety. Most also possessed
too strong an urge to preach, or a desire to reduce the whole
problem down to drugs, religion, family, racism, or some other
narrow agenda. Even more problematic, most viewed educational success or failure as only marginally related to the
behavior of gang members. I, of course, saw it as fundamental.

I finally found a person at Cal State L.A. with whom I felt
comfortable. Juan Esqueda had a sense of humor and a flexible
attitude, enjoyed rascally kids, and shared my view that this
problem involved a broad attack. At 21, he was a year younger
than me and had grown up in a similar East Side neighborhood.
It also helped that his mother made us fat chicken tacos for
lunch every day.

With Juan hired, a grant in hand, some furniture, enough
peanut butter to last a year, and a space to work in, it was time
to look for volunteers. As our neighborhood university, USC was
the logical place to begin recruiting. I called the graduate school
of education, and they put me in contact with a professor
involved in the teacher training program. After one brief meeting, Dr. William Lee volunteered to send me some of his best
student teachers. He worked out a plan that allowed the volunteers to earn credit for participating in the project, even though
it lacked accreditation; * that exposed young interns to some

---

*   Accreditation, of course, signifies that a school, besides being legal, has
also been reviewed by an independent association. All public and
Catholic schools are accredited. The process is hugely expensive, however, and simply wasn't feasible for a small school like ours. The main
drawback to lacking accreditation is that some universities might question the grades of an applicant more so than if they had graduated from
an accredited school. In our case, this was a small consequence for kids
who, up to this time, had little chance of finishing school at all.

rough kids; and that employed the experimental methods of a young person like myself. Dr. Lee had no fear: He thought it would be a good experience for his trainees.

Textbooks, however, were a no go. They would have cost several thousand dollars for each student to have his or her own books for history, math, science, English, and Spanish. Even with the $20-a-month student tuition, our small budget left only a few hundred dollars for supplies. So I went looking for free books. They had to be at various reading levels, with lots of pictures, and touching on as many subjects as possible. These we received from a well-known private school and from L.A.'s Central Public Library.

For the first call, Sharky and I made a trip to the Flintridge Sacred Heart Academy for Girls, an elite boarding school where I helped assemble their elaborate theatrical productions. The head of the drama department made arrangements with the school librarian for me to inherit their used books. When we got there, a tall, beautiful, cordial Asian student helped us around. Obviously affluent and educated, she made quite an impression on both of us. Sharky carried boxes in his gray khakis and starched, oversized T-shirt, bobbing behind her in that funny walk he perfected and now did without thinking.

On the drive back down the hill, he mentioned, "I'd like to have a girlfriend like that *chinita*[†]—clean and, you know, nice."

"You might have to change a few things for a girl like that."

"I know, Homes. It's like my friend, Tomas. In his house, he got all kinds of trophies for him and his dad. Baseball, football."

"You ever play sports?"

"In the projects, they used to take us dirt biking. It was bad, Homes. But I never got no trophies."

Lots of the books from Sacred Heart had titles like *The Secret of Hastings Hill*—with pictures on the cover of tortured-looking girls on windy cliffs—but there were assorted history and science readers as well.

[†] Chinese girl.

To get other books, I went to the central library downtown, where teachers could check out 100 books at a time for an entire semester. I arrived late in the day and was in a hurry—and unfortunately without Sharky this time. I parked about six blocks away—close by downtown standards. I figured they would have some kind of ramp where I could pull up and load the books I picked out. I'd run back to the car and drive back for them—a simple plan.

At the checkout counter, they gave me one huge box and a smaller box to put on top of that. Both were loaded. The library had no ramp to pull up to, and it was near closing, so they needed me out of there with my books. I couldn't leave the books on the sidewalk and expect they would be there when I got back.

I heaved the boxes up on my shoulder, got a few steps, and let the whole thing drop. I put the books back in the boxes and decided I would have to do this in stages. I lifted the big box against my stomach and waddled forward 10 yards, put it down and came back for the little box and brought it past the big box. Then I went back for the big box, did my power lift up to my belly, and staggered up to the little box. I had made it 20 yards from the library. The day gave up on me as the sun slipped over Bunker Hill into West L.A. The boxes were already showing wear from the way I was jerking them around. A box full of books is like a box full of bricks.

I began to think I wasn't in shape to do this all the way back to my car. My arms had gone to jelly in less than a block.

I lifted the big box, this time trying to get it on my shoulder again to see if I could make it further. I gave it one desperate heave, and it suddenly flew, weightless, right past my head. A tall African American man in jeans and a green tank top had taken hold of it and now had it on his shoulder.

"You looked like you needed help. Where are you going?"

"It's pretty far—all the way to Pico. I'm taking these for my students, but it's too heavy for me."

"I've got you."

"Are you sure? I wasn't able to get a few feet at a time with them."

"Allah is my strength, brother."

After a couple of blocks, he was tilting, the weight of the books trying to push him over. But he managed to carry the box all the way to the car, with only occasional help from me as I would free up one arm so I could reach up to give a little support. I was very, very grateful to him.

And to Allah, for keeping an eye out for me.

Rice and Beans: Teaching Gangs in a One-Room School

In Los Angeles, many Mexican restaurants display the portrait of an Aztec warrior bowed on one knee. He holds a dead princess in his arms, and his feathered head faces the Aztec heaven. In one of my earliest memories, my father sits across a restaurant table from my brother and me and explains the meaning of this ancient image:

> Toward the last years of the empire, during the age known in Mexico as *El Quinto Sol*, The Fifth Sun, a warrior and the daughter of an Aztec king fell in love. Although the warrior knew that only a man of royal birth could marry this princess, he nonetheless begged her hand. The young warrior vowed he would face any challenge the king put to him.

> Such a demand had never been made on an Aztec king and would usually have resulted in death for its arrogance. But the king saw an advantage to the warrior's zeal. He proposed to the suitor the following task: "Bring to me the heads of my 10 enemies on your sword, and you will marry my daughter." The king's reasoning was sound. He believed that no warrior could survive this; but in trying, a few of the king's enemies

might perish. And he would rid himself of the warrior's nuisance.

Years passed. The young man disappeared into the vast world of tribes and nations in search of the enemies of his king. The princess waited for his return.

Upon the 12th year of this quest, scouts reported to the king that a warrior approached the great city of Tenochtitlan. He possessed a sword with 10 heads pierced upon it.

But as the Aztecs well knew, the gods are indifferent to man, and each day brings its own battle. The morning the warrior returned, the princess found a viper among the flowers in the palace garden, and its bite killed her.

The warrior asked only one favor of the king—that he be allowed to bury the princess alone and in a place of his own choosing. As was tradition, a high priestess of the temple offered the princess to heaven and, after prayers of mourning, wrapped her in sacred cloth. She was then given to the warrior, who carried her in his arms toward the great volcanic mountains above the city. There he held her upon one knee and begged the heavens to bury them together.

The mountain where he made this plea is still there, but it is very different today than during El Quinto Sol. Before the death of the princess, this high region had little rain and never saw snow. But upon hearing the voice of the warrior, the goddess Tonantsin, the mother of all creation, felt moved and chilled the sky. In time, clouds formed, then rain, and then snow—snow that covered the ground where the warrior held his princess and then, inch over inch, buried them together.

They are still there, under the perpetual snow on this mountain.

On a trip my family made to Mexico City years later, we drove by a pair of mountains surrounded by volcanic rock. We stopped the car, and my father pointed out that the larger mountain had a bent peak at the summit, and this peak overlooked the smaller mountain next to it. "There they are," he said. "The warrior and the princess. Can you see them?" The mountains themselves had assumed the shape of the couple they had entombed.

The world is about stories to me. My parents told them continually. One moment, my mother was telling the tale of how the Virgin of Guadalupe hid my great uncle in her cloak to make him invisible during the revolution. The next, my father was looking up over his science magazine and explaining that

> Everything in the universe is made of the same stuff. We are all made of atoms, and the only difference between a dog's tooth and a dog's tail is how the atoms are stuck together. If you put them together in one shape, they are strong as diamonds. Change their shape, and a diamond becomes water. Your atoms and those in a piece of marble are made of the same bits of energy. An atom is an atom. The only difference is how they are knitted together. If I rearranged your atoms into a different shape, I could turn you into anything— a tortilla or a polyester suit.

Mexican stories mimic our cooking: Fact and fiction, like rice and beans, are stuffed into the same tortilla. But this is how I learned to love learning. I understood sitting with an adult, hearing a story, asking questions, and being guided to thought about them. I didn't understand the undifferentiated droning of schoolbooks and school teachers. To me, my father's chemistry lesson is a story not much different from an Aztec legend. It isn't just a set of facts, but a small tale of how the world is held together.

I knew that, at El Santo Niño, even the least able student would learn if I broke the world into stories like those my father offered. A slow or young student could, at minimum, picture the invisible atoms and recall that everything was made of them. To such a student, I planned to offer a C for comprehending the core of the story. More advanced or older students could go further and get an A or a B for relating additional details about the story of atomic bonding or Aztec history.

In terms of the daily routine at El Santo Niño, the mechanism for this to occur would be simple and repetitive—relating a story to the whole group, then having the students work in small groups under the guidance of volunteer teachers, followed by a whole group discussion, followed by a test (with the questions given beforehand—I don't believe tests should be mysteries). We would move on to new topics when the last student had captured the minimal, main concept necessary for a C and when I felt it was appropriate to finish those aspects of the lesson in which more advanced students had involved themselves.

I knew this would be impossible to do without several teachers on hand. This kind of instruction would require significant adult attention and a generous flexibility with time. This was why I placed a priority on adults in the classroom over textbooks and would have students consistently tutoring other students as part of their own learning. I knew, too, we would have occasional rough landings, as some students would be ready for new things while others needed to stay on certain subjects. But life is a compromise. This system would work better than anything else to keep the slowest students moving forward and the most able pushing their own limits.

When I started El Santo Niño, I believed that learning ignited when three relational events occur between a teacher and a student.

First, the teacher presents a story—not a set of facts or a chronology of events, but a story. The difference is that a story builds to a point of importance, prods the imagination, and makes a point. A story has urgency and meaning for the teacher. It is imbued with intention when delivered to the student. As my father's tales exemplified, this remains true whether a lesson stems from history or chemistry.

Second, something must be physically and mentally manipulated, turned over, looked into, questioned, and picked apart. The student has to interact with the story, while a teacher follows that movement and helps give it shape.

Finally, you have to allow enough time for learning to take place. With a coherent, meaningful story and a sustained, guided struggle, any person can learn just about anything, provided sufficient time. A student's progress, and not the wishes of the curriculum, indicates when sufficient time has been provided.

These three steps applied for me whether the object of scrutiny consisted of an historical narrative or a skill such as factoring numbers or replacing a brake pad. The learning still transpired in that sustained and intent-filled contact among teacher, student, and some point of attention. It still required the teacher to have vision and urgency; to provide a sustained interaction; and, crucially, to allow enough time for the alchemy to ignite.

Those were the principles I consulted when planning for a group of kids who, until now, had not enjoyed school or had success with it.

Roll Call

Pirate, Creeper, Smiley, Sharky, Playboy, Happy, Sad Eyes, Lonely, Psycho, Woody, Droopy, Shadow, Yogi, Spanky, Sparky, Casper, Goofy, Lil Man, Joker, Peanut, Sleepy, Wino, and Sad Girl. That was our opening day crowd.

This was most of the local gang. Of those who didn't show, Popeye was in jail now, and Silent was living in Fresno with an uncle. I had heard that Shorty had moved in with Nikki and her mom in Compton, though I hadn't seen him in months, and that Puppet was pregnant and living in a group home. Tiny had decided she would be fine in the local high school, and I agreed. She had become quite a volleyball player, especially for her size, and wanted to get involved in athletics at Jefferson High School.

Gang members are not from Mars or Venus. Their behavior differs only in degree from expected teenage behavior. They share commonalities that are the reasons for their affiliations, and also differences that account for their idiosyncratic behaviors. They are not brainwashed or automatons. Within the larger group, individuals follow their own prescriptions.

Sharky was 13 and the youngest member of the class. Yogi, who would be 20 soon, was the class senior. The neighbors called it, *"la escuela de los cholitos"*—the school of the little gang members. True, you couldn't get in unless you were a gang member; and except for Lonely, who was from Diamond Street, and Lil Man, who was new in the neighborhood and wouldn't say which gang he was in, you had to be from Primera Flats or Clanton.

The names kids brought with them were not arbitrary. Every kid displayed some characteristic that matched his or her *placa.* * A "Tiny," for example, was usually either very small or really huge. The Tiny in my old neighborhood of Highland Park was a 400-pound mastodon. In this part of town, both Tiny and Peanut held appropriate monikers for petite-size girls. If you were a "Playboy" you had to be good-looking. "Goofy," "Joker," and "Popeye" were names for cutups and clowns; "Wino" and "Psycho," for the stupidly daring.

I had learned by now that each gang member had his or her own reason for the trouble he or she was in. It was never simply a drunken dad, a negligent mom, lack of an after-school job, bad public school teachers, or peer pressure. I knew their parents, and I knew their teachers. In this same neighborhood lived thousands of teenagers with similar backgrounds, who were poor and had family problems, and yet they did not belong to gangs or get into trouble. These gang members were the exception. They had histories of trouble, both at home and in school, but the reasons varied from kid to kid.

Pirate carried with him a painful angst that made him partial to drugs to relieve his pain. He had two hardworking parents who had always involved themselves in his schooling, taken him to Little League, and done all the right things. For his brothers and sisters, it had worked. But for Pirate, all 6-foot-5 of him, it just wasn't enough.

Creeper could not stay still. His body consisted of one thin bone, and he had a "lazy eye" on his left side.† He was as squirmy and as hard to hold as a fish. His grandfather, who was raising him, was trying, but it wasn't enough.

Smiley had a good heart and loved to dream, just like his brothers. But his mind had difficulty keeping things in order. At

---

*   Literally, a badge; in this case, the nickname given each by the gang.

†   Amblyopia, or lazy eye, often occurs among low-income children. Characterized by blurred vision, especially in one eye, the condition is often treated by covering or putting drops into the good eye to blur its vision—thus forcing the weaker eye to work harder and strengthen.

15, he hadn't learned to add simple numbers, even though he had a sister in college and successful, blue-collar parents.

Sharky, who was born in this country, simply couldn't read. He was not dumb, and he had nine years of school behind him, yet he struggled to complete the alphabet or sound out a syllable for me.

Playboy was a smart, articulate, good-looking student. A standout among these boys, he was bored and needed to be reigned in and better occupied.

At 15, Happy moved through life daydreaming, drinking, and scared of the bullets that followed him as he rode his bike home. He was a good-hearted, clueless, girth of a kid. His parents often came over and thanked me for working with him. "He's a good boy, just confused," they would tell me.

Best friends, Sad Eyes and Lonely were two bright girls bored with public school and attracted to gang boys. But they were not the type of girls to be victimized. They considered themselves cholas, but they also had aspirations, and they didn't get mixed up with the drug culture beyond the kind of experimentation typical of many teenagers.

Psycho wasn't mean, but he was like a giant, muscle-bound 8-year-old. Before he knew it, he would do something stupid and be in lots of trouble. He needed self-control, and lots of it. He walked home naked one day when Sad Eyes's brothers waited for him after school, gave him a thrashing, and took his pants—payback for impulsively pawing Sad Eyes in class. He was sorry a few minutes after he did it, but too late to pacify her family.

Woody was a typical bad boy with poor academics, but he also had a work ethic gained from helping nights in his father's janitorial business. A young man on the verge of insight and maturity, he just needed a bit of catching up and, like most teenagers, some mentoring from someone who wasn't his parent.

Droopy could fix television sets, had two siblings on the way to college, and made great company and conversation. But he had a fuse in one hand and a blow torch in the other. Once angry, nothing mattered, and only regrets followed. His addiction to paint made it worse. He was always good when he was with me or with a relative, but this couldn't be all of the time. Regular public school—where they gave him a seat for an hour and got in his face if he moved—created an impossible situation for him. The local school wouldn't take him back since he beat up a teacher. I rarely had problems with him, but I understood how he was geared, and I had the flexibility to shift my expectations when necessary.

Shadow, Sharky's older brother, was an example of the typical slow learner, the mildly retarded. He loved juvenile hall because of the discipline of prison life and the fact that, in the jail school, everyone worked at their own pace. Outside of juvenile hall, he spent his time high on paint and quietly following the other boys around.

Yogi moved like the big bear he resembled—6-foot-4 and over 200 pounds—but he was never violent and not a drug user. All the boys liked him. He was a very peripheral gang member who had dropped out of school in the seventh grade and was running an auto painting business out of his parents' front yard. He belonged to the gang because they were the only kids he could hang out with during the day.

Spanky frustrated teachers. He was a 14-year-old with the maturity of 7-year-old. He was not dangerous, but lazy, a bit spoiled, and childish. As a rule, he would stare at a teacher all year without ever putting a pencil to paper. He seldom passed a class.

Sparky, like Playboy, had smarts, never engaged in violence, and seldom went beyond moderation in drug use. He was a genuine businessman: Unlike the other gang members, he made serious money in the drug market and knew how to save it. He was a busy guy and didn't have time for the other boys' shenanigans.

Casper's father pastored a small local church. Casper suffered a heavy addiction to paint, sherm sticks, and alcohol, but was always helpful and polite. Like Happy, he had a fundamental intelligence that had never been tapped but that required constant refocusing and reworking of the school material. Otherwise, he just sat passively vacant and retained nothing in class. He was a sweet boy but was still very willing to get in your face if he felt put down or threatened.

The school psychologist at Adams had assessed Goofy as having an above-average IQ. He possessed a subtle sense of humor, but also a learning disability that prevented him from exercising his gifts. He spent his days, morning till evening, stoned at the park, staring at the sky and talking nonsense—hence, the name Goofy.

Lil Man scowled all the time. He was a small, angry African American kid who always wore a blue cap that shielded his eyes and squashed his curls. Completely illiterate, and scared of anyone finding out, he was a sweet, no-nonsense kid when he wasn't being threatened.

Joker, like Yogi, limited his participation in the gang to the movies, partying, and kicking around with some of the boys. Of noble character, and not violent or criminal, he had an aging mother to take care of and had dropped out of school at a young age to work. His drug use never went beyond something remedied by *menudo** and Tabasco sauce the next morning.

Peanut measured only 4-foot-6 at age 15. She was a slight, pretty girl with long black hair who paid attention to nothing but boys. Most days, getting Peanut out of bed involved a

---

* *Menudo* is tripe, the stomach lining of a cow. It is a Mexican breakfast dish. You boil it all night. No one really gets used to the smell, but you learn to sleep through it. It has hominy in it and is served with lemon, oregano, onions, and chili over the top. It has a chewy, slippery texture that takes practice to enjoy.

† Camps are run by the California Youth Authority (CYA) and by local juvenile authorities as well. CYA camps tend to have tight security, whereas local camps depend on their distance from the cities to discourage runaways. Kids do go AWOL frequently, however. If the escape is impulsive, the runaways are usually caught a few miles down the road. If the escape is planned, and the kids have arranged for some kind of ride to pick them up, then catching up with them takes a bit longer.

protracted struggle between her and her mother. Because she lived only a couple of doors from the school, we could hear the volleys as her mother shoved her out the door

Sleepy was Peanut's brother. Almost ambitious, and possessing a snide sense of humor, he asked on the first day of class, "At our prom, do we all dance with Sad Eyes and Lonely?" He dressed well, worked when pressed, but could be a real jerk at times.

Wino, a Puerto Rican transplant from New York, told me as soon as he showed up, "I'm dumb. I didn't even finish first grade. I don't know nothin' about school. The police didn't even try to find me when I went AWOL from camp.[†] They knew I would do something stupid and they would just catch me."

Sad Girl was living in a foster home after having been molested by a brother-in-law. Her parents were in El Salvador. Her foster mother had put her in a church group which had improved her behavior. Feeling very alone, she had run through a series of boyfriends, and her foster mother feared she was simply trying to get pregnant.

What bound these teens as a group was that, for reasons from boredom to poverty to mild retardation, they had all slipped out of the net and were now floundering. In other circumstances, the very bright ones would have been working toward scholarships in programs for gifted students, the ones with learning disabilities would have received the help they needed, some who were bored would have been offered alternative education programs, the emotionally taxed and addicted would have had access to counseling, and the low-income students would have been offered some options to combine school with work. For many reasons, all had let go of the community's—our community's—towline to adulthood. And, being children, they simply stayed stranded, got into trouble, and made things much worse for themselves.

PART THREE

A Village School for the Children of the Gang

Sharky and Lil Man Learn to Read

Sharky struggled with the alphabet, and reading went something like, "The . . . ho . . . horse . . . house . . . for . . . what's this word?"

"Sharon. It's a name."

"I don't understand this story. It don't make sense."

Lil Man was worse than Sharky. He knew the first half of the alphabet, but after that it got dicey. He had no idea of how to put a vowel and consonant together to make a syllable. He was from one of the African American gangs in Watts, but neither the kids nor I knew anything more about it than that. Eighteenth Street was the monster gang everyone here worried about. Bloods and Crips we never thought about. Lil Man didn't make an issue of it. After only two weeks at the local high school, the principal had expelled him and put him on OT. He was supposed to take a bus to the Metro Continuation School downtown. His grandfather didn't think he would go, so he had signed him up here, "where the Mexican boys who cause trouble go."

Nietzsche said, "Nothing is as expensive as a start." Starting is slow, and foundations take time; but as they firm up, it becomes possible to make time and even catch up with those who got out of the gate with a better step. So I sat with Lil Man and Sharky after school and said, "You guys can't read, and that's not your fault. Nobody's taken the time to teach you. I'm going to teach you to read well. It'll take about half the year. To get an 'A,' your job is to learn to read. Everyone's got a goal—that'll be yours. If you don't learn, then I don't know what I'm doing."

I typed out three sheets with simple phonetic combinations of vowels and consonants—hundreds of them. The first sheet began with the syllables, "co, co, la, la, da, da, ba, ba, be, be. . . ." I put it in front of them, and said, "Follow me." After a few minutes of that, I placed a simple book in front of them, and we read together. I took the lead on these exercises quickly and with conviction, so there was little opportunity for complaints or embarrassment. They read out loud throughout the day after that, always with someone listening.

Yogi was good for that. He lived behind the school and came over to brush up on the basics, maybe get a diploma, explore what else might be out there for him. He would sit and listen to them read; so did Sad Eyes or Lonely, and sometimes Droopy or Smiley, once it became normal to hear their staccato, struggling voices in the background. As the class got used to it, a tired or bored student would ask to go listen to Sharky or Lil Man read awhile.

One day in January, the class was drawing the organs of the body, Spanky and Casper were with Juan going over the globe and matching countries to pictures from *National Geographic,* and Sharky was reading about how the slaves were brought on ships and sold. From his end of the picnic table, Sharky blew out a perfect set of notes: "Many people died on the ships." He stopped and glanced up at me. "I don't read all slow and stopping anymore, ay Homes?" He looked a little startled with himself.

"No, you don't. You got it down, Sharky."

Lil Man never gave that kind of proclamation. As he gained competence, he began lifting his cap back so he could look you in the eye, and started fighting the other students for a seat nearer the front of the class.

* * * * *

An 8-year-old girl from the Jordan Downs housing project received attention in the newspapers several years ago. She held a one-room play school in the housing project's recreation center, and her young students had improved remarkably in their reading levels.

I picture her in a circle of children, listening, correcting, directing them to read a sentence again "the right way." That's what an 8-year-old would probably do.

Why is that so hard for us?

15

Birds on a Wire, or Smiley Puts Two and Two Together

There are kids in gangs who do violence to others and to themselves; and there are those who fear it, who are shy, apathetic, and scared. They are shadows in the gang, neither stopping nor participating in the violence.

Smiley had dreams. He was curious and kind. Other gang members were "destructive," which unsettled him. I remember fondly that he made a bench of wood crates for us to sit on while I waited for the bus after school. He hid it behind a tree and would pull it out when he walked me to the bus stop at the end of the day.

One afternoon, I had to close the Catholic community center, where I worked in the evenings, to rush his dog to the vet. He had asked a neighbor to clip the little mutt's ears so it would look mean, like a Doberman. But by the time I got there, the dog was butchered and bleeding to death under a tree where Smiley had placed it.

"I want to save its life," he told me. We drove to the vet, who had to put the dog to sleep. The vet told me, "I see many of these things, and they're awful. But if I went to court or got into each case, I'd have no time to help animals or keep my business. You know what I mean." I was angry about the dog, and he was letting me know that he wasn't into pursuing it.

Smiley was full of regrets. "I didn't know, Homie. You know, I just wanted it to look tough. I didn't know, Homie. The man told me he knew how to cut ears. He jacked up my dog."

Smiley had two siblings in college, a third who played in a band, and two hardworking, decent parents. They owned a home that had been carefully maintained. Yet no one, not in school or at home, had noticed that Smiley was completely uneducated, that schooling had left no trace on him. He was unable to do any mathematics at all, nothing requiring more addition than could be done on his fingers. He could not give you any historical facts or the name of the planet he inhabited. Yet he was in the ninth grade and had attended the local elementary and junior high school. He had learned to hide, to manage impressions with kindness and cleverness.

Until recently, I thought this only happened in inner cities, but my friend Ami Kern, a scholar in rhetoric and a performance artist, told me that she was illiterate until the sixth grade, when a teacher finally busted her. "They made me go to a special school," she told our philosophy discussion group one evening, somewhat embarrassed. "I learned how to copy, and I listened really well so that it seemed I knew what was going on. Even when they sent me to the school, I still tried not to learn. They had to keep changing the way they taught me so that I had to read and couldn't cheat. Now I read a novel a week."

When Smiley began the year at El Santo Niño, he could read at about a fourth- or fifth-grade level, which, except for Playboy and Pirate, was exceptional for the group. In Smiley's case, literacy was not problematic. His biggest and fundamental deficit was math. In the same way that Lil Man and Sharky hardly knew their alphabets when they started, Smiley could do no arithmetic except count on his fingers. He could not add simple equations in his head or on paper.

Watching Smiley struggle with arithmetic, I learned much about the relation of one mental process with the others. Smiley obviously had intelligence, and he was observant. When I had to go to court over a problem with a landlord, he advised me to take a lawyer with me.

"I can't afford one."

"Anybody with a suit and a briefcase, Homeboy. He just has to look like one."

And he could read. So why the lack of knowledge? Apparently, his inability to hold numbers in head and to understand a concept like multiplication also hampered his efforts to put together other kinds of information. He knew about the world in bits, but they did not come together into wholes that made sense. He knew about Earth, and he knew he lived on a planet. He just didn't know that Earth was the planet he lived on. Smiley had difficulty putting two and two together when it involved listening to strings of information.

The only solution to his difficulty with numbers was to imagine what it would be like to think like him, and then to invent a method of guided imagery that would train Smiley away from his fingers when counting. We worked on addition and subtraction for months, and then multiplication and division for months.

The daily routine began with birds: "Smiley, close your eyes and imagine five pigeons."

"Where are they?"

"On a telephone wire. Have one fly away. Can you picture the ones that are still on the wire?"

Guiding his thought processes in this direct manner proved to be the needed therapy. In time, numbers became a part of him, and he could manipulate and order the things in the world the way that only math allows. By year's end, he was picking up fractions with ease—his mind had developed a facility with this process of breaking the world into pieces that he could move around and reassemble.

"I couldn't even do two plus two before I came here," he told his mother when she thought about pulling him out of the school.

Of course, this new skill affected other areas as well. He had learned to put together disparate pieces of information and see their relatedness. This gave him an interest in history and Chicano politics, which he developed into an avid hobby.

Like all basic learning, the beginning was tedious, frustrating, and laborious—drills out loud, drills on paper, and constant guided practice. It took several weeks before anything significant occurred. But after the first insight, followed another; and when he had finally disciplined his mind to hold numbers constant and to manipulate them, he learned math without further difficulty and the world became a more accessible place to him.

* * * * *

When I was working on the Pima-Maricopa reservation, my colleagues and I once argued about whether certain students had genuine learning disabilities or just lacked motivation. The director of education intervened and informed us forcefully that lack of motivation, if it prevented a student from learning, was obviously a disabling condition for the student. It was real and had to be attended to.

Playboy Meets the Buddha

There were days when we ran out of things to do, or we could see that the kids or the teachers needed a break. Those days, we'd make sandwiches from the stuff we had in the kitchen, crowd into the van,* and take trips to museums, a movie, or a part of town to explore.

Other trips were better planned. We went to places in L.A. that would flesh out ideas. Since we had been covering history and world religions, I contacted Buddhist monasteries, Jewish synagogues, Greek Orthodox churches, and Indian museums, and made an itinerary.

Pirate decided to skip the trip and go home. He was in a horrid mood. He could be a pain, so I wasn't going to push it. He was verbal and bright and could have performed decently in a public school, except he was always angry, wouldn't work, and was stoned most the time. His parents had brought him to El Santo Niño. They were involved in the community and had heard about the school. They warned me he would be stubborn. The first few weeks, he mostly came to class and went to sleep on the benches that lined the auditorium's walls, taking part in a discussion now and then by raising his head and arguing a

---

* I had recovered my van, stripped of everything but frame and engine. The boys helped me put some carpet in it. After a little rewiring and tinkering, it was hardy enough to serve as a school bus.

point for a minute. We allowed it, as pushing him had only frustrated everyone else in his life.

You would think that allowing Pirate to get away with this would have set off a rebellion—and, in fact, one kid tried to mimic him and sleep on the wall. But he wasn't serious; he got a quick "don't even try it" talk. Kids are smart. They could see that Pirate had a problem and that this was why he received different treatment. Kids know the difference between unfair and special situations.

So Pirate did his routine for a few weeks. When we didn't fight with him or put him down, he got so bored that he gradually participated in more of the school day, began to find it rewarding, and eventually was participating like everyone else. But today, he was in one of those moods, and I wasn't going to beg him.

Sharky compulsively drew on things, including my van if I didn't watch him. He was always apologetic and willing to scrub it off; but prevention was better, so I made him empty his pockets before getting in. At UCLA, the placaso he drew on the parking lot cost us $50. "Sorry Homes," he said, "My hand just starts making the neighborhood." *

Our first stop was the beautiful Greek Orthodox cathedral, St. Sophia, with its huge dome from which Mary looks down from a Byzantine sky. The kids were reverent enough and understood that this was similar to a Catholic church but with a different pope. The long-bearded priest saying, "Hello," to them left an image to which they could attach the word *Greek*. The Virgin Mary painted across the dome was impressive to them as the biggest mural they had ever seen.

At a small synagogue in the Fairfax district, a rabbi discussed the Holocaust with them. A group of Orthodox men came in with their long coats and beards, which fascinated them, and helped the rabbi with the presentation. The one question they really wanted to ask, though—about their dress

---

* "Making the neighborhood" is gang lingo for doing graffiti. To the gang kids, placasos and graffiti symbols are synonymous with the neighborhood. The act of graffiti "makes" or extends the neighborhood.

and appearance—they held back on. Usually, they might have been willing to be a bit rude and stir things up a little, but after the Holocaust lecture, all the kids were a little sensitized.

We had lunch at Canter's deli down the street. I ordered the least expensive thing on the menu, a round of matzo ball soup for the group. Here, they asked me immediately, "So why did those guys all dress like Abraham Lincoln?" I really had no idea, but we all thought it was pretty cool looking. The soup filled us up, even though each bowl had just one big meatball in it.

For the Buddhist experience, we stopped at an old, two-story house in East Hollywood that served as a monastery. Thomas, an American convert, met us in the parking lot and told us that the priest would meet us in the meditation room upstairs. In the large atrium, we sat on mats in a circle, our backs against the wall.

"You think Homeboy's going to do kung fu?" Casper wondered out loud.

Trying to get comfortable, Thomas asked, "You all come from the same school?"

"Yeah," Joker said. "From Gangster High."

"Have some *respeto,*† fool," Casper shot back. To Thomas, he said, "*Dispense,*‡ he don't know how to act."

They were used to talking to each other that way, so it didn't escalate.

Thomas continued, ignoring them, "Master Ong is a Buddhist monk. Do you have ideas about what that might be?"

"It's like from China," Sad Eyes offered.

Sharky added, "They believe in reincarnation, or something like that, Homey."

"Like when you come back as animals 'cause you're bad," Goofy extended, "and you pray to the Buddha man."

Thomas smiled, satisfied with their answers. "That's all correct. It looks like you've been studying."

I felt pretty good. They were giving a decent account of themselves.

---

†   Respect.

‡   Pardon, forgive, or excuse.

The Master appeared in a black robe with something like meditation or rosary beads at his waist. He was Chinese, short, probably in his 50s, with a shaved head, and he walked with a cane. He bowed to the kids, some of whom sort of bowed backed from their seats. Thomas introduced him, "This is Master Ong. He is the monk who leads this monastery."

Playboy made a crack, and the monk immediately responded, "You speak again no permission and I hit your back 40 times." He was obviously aware of the popularity of the television show *Kung Fu* and that the students would associate him with it. The threat was enough to calm them down. He had a good sense of humor.

"Master Ong can see an object coming from behind," Thomas explained. "He reacts in a moment because he is always in the present."

The monk cut him off. "I teach you Buddhism. What is this?" He tapped on the floor with his cane.

"It's the floor," the group mumbled, knowing something was up.

"No, that's it's name. What is it?"

Playboy decided to engage him. "It's wood."

"That's the material it is made from. What is it?"

"You walk on it," Playboy answered with more energy.

"That is its function. What is it?" He tapped with his cane on the floor several times.

"It's whatever you think it is," Lonely came back.

"So what is it?" Psycho was losing patience.

"It is," responded the monk, tapping again on the floor.

"The sound?" several students asked at once.

"No." Master Ong shook his head.

"I get it," Playboy said. "It just is."

Master Ong regarded him. "If you understand, you will be happy." With that, the monk stood, excused himself, and bowed again to us.

Thomas walked us back outside after showing us some artifacts and explaining their use. "This is a good thing for peace you're doing," he told me.

Never Far from Home

Home is the place where, when you have to go there,
they have to take you in.

Robert Frost

The brown paper bag, the spray can, and the rag were Shadow's trademarks. Even on public transportation, Shadow got high. He always went straight to the bench seat at the back of the bus. There, he would shake the can concealed in a paper bag, rattling the little ball inside, and pump a thick, close-range spray into the rag he always carried in his pocket. He then pressed the wet rag to his face and inhaled deeply. The result was a silver-faced boy in a stupor. I often saw him staggering off the bus in this state.

In class, he learned very slowly, and I couldn't tell if he had always been this way or if the glues and paints had degenerated his abilities. Much of the time, he just stared at me, and unless the work I gave him had a visible repetitive structure, he couldn't do it.

When Shadow disappeared one morning, Juan took a drive at lunch to look for him. He found him wandering the neighborhood, incoherent and smelling of paint. Juan called me from a pay phone outside the corner store on Maple and 30th. "Arturo, guess what I found? I got Shadow in the car. What should I do with him?"

"Is he pretty messed up?"

"He's just sitting and twitching his face. I pulled up next to him, and he just got in the car. He's in a good mood, but he's stuttering so bad he can't talk."

"I think we need to do something while he still has some brain left."

"I'll take him home," Juan offered.

"Meet me at El Tepeyec in Hollenbeck after you drop him off. We'll have a burrito and think about this."

I called his probation officer later that afternoon and said I would testify that Shadow was out getting stoned and was not attending school as his probation demanded. I didn't have to do much convincing. The PO asked me what I thought he needed, and I said lots of structure and a safe place to be sober for a few months.

So Shadow was picked up and taken to juvenile hall.

The kids knew I had something to do with this, and yet no one, not even his little brother Sharky, expressed anger over it. Even gang members like to see their friends alive and healthy, and all of us knew that Shadow's time on earth would be short if he continued anesthetizing himself in solvents all day. But their acceptance also relied on the knowledge that Shadow remained one of us.

I visited Shadow once a month, and the kids sent him letters. I asked his teacher at juvenile hall to keep me abreast of his progress and to let him know of my continued interest. I sent notes with his mother wishing him well and letting him know I was looking forward to having him back.

Several months later, he returned, 20 pounds heavier, and praising the juvenile hall school. "They're strict there, and you have to go to school every day or you can't leave your room. I learned a lot in there."

And so he came back, and we went on with him. I tried to create a structure for him that was easier to follow, closer to what he enjoyed at the hall, and I tried to find support for sobriety in a therapist intern who visited us twice a week from the local university.

For the time being, the combined effects of incarceration and our efforts helped keep him steady. If he had required it, I would have sent him away again. Had the school lasted longer, I am sure another relapse would have occurred. That is the nature of addiction—it has to be expected and planned for. At that point, I would have looked for some place, maybe juvenile hall again, that could have protected and helped him with resources that neither his school, neighborhood, nor family could provide. In time, the periods between relapses would have become longer, and eventually the addiction would have turned into a threat he could manage. That, too, is the nature of addiction. This is true especially when the addict is a teenager and the adult response is both strong and consistent.

Shadow knew that incarceration remained at ready disposal in terms of keeping him straight. But there is all the difference in the world between being sent away and being abandoned. His school, his PO, and his family used the former as tool in a joint struggle to raise a struggling youth. But we claimed him as our own. Our eyes would be on him, and the adult community to which he belonged would always welcome him.

That's what being a homeboy is really all about.

I Lean on Casper and Sharky

El Santo Niño called to kids who simply went into overload in the public schools. In our school, there was no failure, and there were no "good kids" to have to compete with. The exaggerated, the rigid, is always a way to compensate, a way to divert attention and harm from a more fragile part of ourselves. In this place, though, nothing was attacking them, and they didn't need to be tough.

When students were belligerent, it was usually because I had lost sight of this. When that happened, the kids knew they were being pinned and asked to do what they could not.

Casper started school like all of them—illiterate and full of attitude. Like many of these boys, you didn't feed him fastballs. You gave him big, fat slow balls and let him get some wood on them. By our taking it slow, repeating things, and being patient, Casper began to experience the feel of learning and the pleasure of discovering he could get a handle on this world. By December, he was swinging for the fences and enjoying the tests—a polite, diligent student.

Playboy had found a job through his brother at a Kentucky Fried Chicken in Beverly Hills. The owner liked his work, so when Playboy brought Casper in for an interview, the owner hired him immediately. By end of the month, gang members were frying chicken, working the register, cleaning the bathrooms, and politely asking if people wanted biscuits or coleslaw.

The last one hired was Happy. It was his first job, and the day of the interview he sat in class petrified all morning and afternoon. He was even worse the first day of work. But he caught on.

The boys watched each other and made sure no one stole anything. Since Playboy was an assistant manager, he kept the others in line. The owner, whom I never met, knew they were all gang members, and it was a very good thing he was doing with them.

In February, Happy quit. He came to class one day and said that it was too many hours and he had to concentrate on his education. He was a hefty boy, with a thin mustache that made him look like a Greek fisherman. He had often told me that when he got high, he just started running and sometimes went for a mile or two, and that it felt free. He had an innocence that didn't match his size, and my heart was warmed to hear him walk in with his pressed T-shirt and talk about the importance of an education over a part-time job.

Casper was also working long hours, sometimes closing during the week and getting home at 1:00 or 2:00 in the morning. He started missing school, but it was obvious the money was helping him and his family. I had been so happy with his previous work that I leaned on him about missing school, told him he had to be on time or he couldn't come at all. It was stupid of me. We had developed a mutual admiration, and now there was this adversarial quality to our relationship. He got an attitude because I got an attitude.

He opted for the job and decided to skip the school; but he kept coming around occasionally, trying to sit in, saying he could pass our tests, wanting his grades. It wasn't a clean break.

What I should have done was work around the fact that he was coming home late and therefore getting up late. I could have assigned him extra take-home work; given him partial but important credit for a partial day; or tailored the curriculum, using the experience as a lesson in problem solving, choices, endurance, and managing competing concerns. It could have been a rite of passage, if I had been able to mentor this smartly.

Instead, I took it personally rather than as one more turn with which a mentor needed to accompany him. I didn't need to box him in.

A kid doesn't mind rigidity when you're mentoring and not fighting him. When Sharky didn't show for several days, his classmates took me to where he was staying. It was early in the morning, and I walked into a living room where he was sleeping with a woman 10 years older than him. Her brothers were sleeping in the same room. I was mad and told Sharky, "You better get outside unless you want me to get someone in this room for statutory rape."

He was startled and for a few seconds was caught between pulling up his pants and making that forward jerk with the arms and shoulders that means, "Come on, do something about it." It looked like a mime dance. He came outside, acted mad for a few seconds, then took his tongue lashing and admitted he should have come by and discussed this. He was apologetic.

I was wrong about the woman. He was 14, and she was 24 and had two children; but 15 years later they were still together, and he was making a decent father.

If You Build It...

Not only did the gang kids gravitate to the school quickly and naturally, but so did people in the community who wanted to help.

Therapist interns from Cal State L.A. appeared at our door one morning asking if they could volunteer some hours. At 22, I had never met anyone who had been to therapy, so I wasn't sure what occurred in therapy. But I assumed it to be salubrious. They set up in my office for a few hours twice a week, and the kids could choose to go in and talk to them. Happy came out of the room on one occasion, pulled me aside, and told me in a low tone, "The lady says I can talk about anything. I said, 'Even about you and me making . . . making sex?' And she didn't get mad. She said we could even talk about that! Homeboy, I never talked to no lady like this."

At the least, the interns let them know that seeing a therapist might be a pleasant experience and didn't mean you were crazy. It was one more place to get help.

The student teachers from USC worked out great, and the kids loved them. One student teacher was very interested in the kids, so she gave them a lot of time. She was also very voluptuous. Several had crushes on her. They couldn't understand why I wasn't making a move. "Art's afraid of that stuff," they liked to chorus after she would leave.

Help came from many quarters. Officers from the Newton Division of the L.A. Police Department patrolled the local area and knew our gang members. The officers stopped by often and complimented the kids on their progress. The cholos felt good being talked to this way by police officers. It contrasted with their usual conversations, in which the boys would stand in a row at Trinity Park with their heads down, an officer in front of them asking questions, and the gang members all repeating, "I don't know anything, I didn't see anything," a mutual, ritualistic ordeal played out daily between the cholos and the police. Being complimented by the police and having a chance to be nice kids admired by important adults—well, this was new and enjoyable.

Interestingly, most of the gang kids wanted to be police officers when they grew up. They knew that, with their records, this was an impossible wish, but it was a wish nonetheless. Police work represented goodness, strength, and respect, qualities for which all people have some yearning. Understandably, this yearning prevailed in kids who knew they had been a real letdown to their parents and community.

The police also sponsored a Police Explorers group—a type of scout troop, except they received a police-issued Explorer uniform. Explorers took field trips, helped out at the station, and worked crowd control at sporting events. A couple of the gang members joined the group, and it made a strong impact on them.

Other organizations helped as well. The local Catholic school gave us some used eighth-grade desks and a stack of report cards so we could send grades home. The local elementary school offered the use of its new photocopier. This gift edged along the law in terms of a public school allowing free use of its equipment to our private school, but the principal was generous and community-minded. The Sugar Ray Robinson Youth Foundation waived its rule about funding only public schools and sponsored a soccer team at our little cholo academy.

Al Rendon, the community affairs director at L.A. Trade Tech, the local junior college, gave us the use of their soccer field for the Sugar Ray team. He also paid us a visit and talked to the kids about junior college. Yogi, who was old enough, went to see him and signed up for the mechanics training program. Yogi took Big Sleepy, who was not in our school but who had an extraordinary artistic talent, to the junior college with him on his second visit. Big Sleepy took a picture of the mural he had completed for the neighborhood butcher, and Mr. Rendon helped him enroll in the commercial design program.

Sister Duran from Catholic Charities took on Smiley and Droopy, who didn't qualify for work through the CETA program because of probation or something, and told them that if they wanted to work, she'd figure something out. They worked for two months without knowing if they were going to get any money, but she managed to pull a couple hundred dollars out of petty cash and her own pocket for them. It was their first job.

And, of course, KFC hired several of our students. Serving the hungry of Beverly Hills and the West Side, the restaurant wasn't in our neighborhood, so driving to work took 30 minutes. But the kids gave each other rides, and parents pitched in when needed.

The Child Guidance Center accepted Goofy for a short time and did a wonderful job with him. Woody came in one day and said he had just seen Goofy at the park. "He was just laying there looking up. He wasn't even high. That's the first time I've seen him like that."

Father Fitzpatrick sent one of his volunteers to help us form our own chapter of *Los Hermanos Unidos* [The Brothers United]. The Father had started these clubs for gang members at several churches. The kids got special jackets and insignia in exchange for vowing to work for unity instead of violence. They took field trips, met with other clubs, attended retreats, held dances, worked toward sobriety, and generally tried to provide an alternative peer group to gang members.

Even Mayor Tom Bradley offered help. His "Task Force on Youth" encouraged several of my students to think seriously about politics. The task force consisted of young people who met on one of the top floors of city hall late on Wednesday nights and advised one of the mayor's deputies on issues related to youth. We rode the elevator with the mayor on a few occasions, and for meetings we got to sit in big chairs around a huge, polished table. There were no field trips or uniforms, but it made the gang members who participated feel important.

Beyond organizations and benefactors, of top importance was the help that came in the form of relationships with judges and probation officers. As they got to know me, we were able to work together so that the gang kids understood we were, in fact, a community looking out for them and not just a bunch of fragmented adults they could keep dodging. Our students knew that I spoke to both their parents and their probation officers, and that all of us discussed their progress. On top of that, if court dates became necessary, students knew that judges usually asked what I thought was best and often took my advice.

Cooperative parents and willing community members were not difficult to find. All we had to do was take a disparate group of adults and put them in touch with each other such that they functioned as a community. The employers, the judges, the parents, the educators, the researchers, the ministers, the police officers, the coaches: We became a village to each other, with a sense of common purpose.

Lonely and Playboy Nearly Take the Town

One of my favorite memories from El Santo Niño was an annual speech competition for junior high students in the public schools, sponsored by the Optimist Oratorical Society. Participants compete for local, regional, state, and national titles in an eliminatory series. I had been in this as a kid and called to see if we could enter. Once I explained the nature of our school, they were excited to have us. I asked Playboy and Lonely to compete in the men's and women's divisions. They were both cocky and verbal and had dreams of becoming lawyers or executives in the fuzzy way that 15-year-olds think of these things.

We worked and reworked their speeches, timed them, and rehearsed them for weeks. The day of the contest, I put on my suit and drove to the school. Lonely had on an elegant, dark dress. It was time to leave, and Playboy came huffing in his suit saying that he couldn't go, that there was going to be a fight and he had to be there, that the fight was important and he couldn't let the gang down.

Of course, there was no big fight. He was just scared, as I remembered being when I had been in the contest. One thing about this kind of exceptional gang member: They're arrogant but insecure. You have to push them, support them, and take no nonsense. I told him he had better cut out the bullshit and take care of the business at hand.

We got to the competition. It was in a rented room in a nice hotel. Of course, the other kids competing were the best the public schools had to offer—student body presidents, leadership types. The judges knew this, and when they introduced Lonely and Playboy, they did so with interest and a certain nice deference, knowing this was a very difficult thing for them.

The other orators were excellent, as they had to be.

Playboy's turn came first. I pressed his shoulder, and Sad Eyes, who had come along to be supportive, whispered, "You'll be all right."

He was amazing. He started stiff-shouldered and speaking too fast, but he caught himself, and from midpoint on, he was animated and only looked at his notes to guide himself, not getting stuck on them as I had feared. The audience loved him as he delivered his speech, "I Am a Gang Member." He walked back looking like he'd made it through a minefield. I was so glad I had forced him to go through with this.

"How was I, Homeboy?"

"Everybody loved it. You've got a good chance."

Lonely was the last of the women's division, and the last of the evening, so she was plenty nervous. She followed a demure girl from Bethune Junior High who gave a polished, well-choreographed speech. You could tell she was comfortable in these settings. Lonely, who was a big girl, and even in a dress looked tough, squeezed my hand as she got up. "Wish me luck, Arturo." Her speech was just as good as the girl's before her, and she knew it. She was a woman victorious when she came back to her seat.

The limit was three minutes; unfortunately, both Lonely and Playboy went over by 10 or 15 seconds, and that cost them points. But they each took second in their divisions and received great applause and the acknowledgment that they might have taken first if not for the time. I wished I had asked their parents to come. They collected their trophies and certificates, and we left the auditorium, after some handshakes and congratulations, into a fine March evening.

Playboy said, "Let's go somewhere good for dinner, a nice place. What about it Art?"

"If everyone wants to."

"I'll treat everyone," he offered.

"How about me and you treat," I countered.

"That's cool, Homeboy."

So the four of us went to a restaurant in Pasadena and enjoyed a late dinner and good conversation. We drove home feeling fed and accomplished.

When Woody Left the Gang
(and No One Noticed)

How hard was it to leave the gang?

Like I said before, gang kids are not from Mars. They have the same troubles in their relationships that we all have. When a young person is ready to leave a set of friends, to end those relationships, it's because that child has changed so much that those friends no longer meet a need and that child has replaced those friends with a new set of people who do. This takes time— as anyone knows who has gone through the kind of changes where you gradually find you want a new mate, new friends, or new relations with family.

The reason why the myth about gangs being hard to leave is popular is because people listen to kids who say, "I want to leave, but they won't let me," just as they listen to friends who say, "I want to break up, but she or he won't let me." We know that the "won't let" is in the heart, not in the other person.

Most gang kids never get the sustained adult support necessary to make a real, deep-seated change, such that they find they no longer really relate to their old friends. When they do, the relationship ends the same way that other relationships end: Both parties leave each other, with a bit of nostalgia and regret.

One of the boys at El Santo Niño was tall and muscular for his age. He was a bit of a bad ass in the gang. Woody didn't show up for the first three weeks at my school because a rival gang had jumped him and left him for dead. When he came in, his arm was still in a cast and his jaws were wired shut so that he had to talk through his teeth.

This event began a transformation for him. Being that near death, turning 16, and going through that pain made him momentarily reflective and started him questioning his vulnerability and whether he wanted to be in that kind of life. This introspection would have gone nowhere, however, without the school. With no path other than the one he knew, he would have eventually returned to the familiar. This happens to all of us when we have big experiences but no immediate avenues that allow us to roll the experiences into long-term changes.

With the school there, however, and with his newfound openness, he learned quickly. As were most of the students, Woody was nearly illiterate, unable to write except in an unpunctuated ramble, and he knew little of the outside world. But now he learned quickly. Soon, he was writing essays, which he actually enjoyed. It had never occurred to him that "writing had an order that made sense," as he put it. He grew increasingly curious about the world; science; countries, and their languages, religions, and customs.

At midyear, he had a beautiful, hardworking girlfriend who wasn't in the gang. His braces came off and, deciding he wanted to go to a regular high school, he transferred to Jefferson. Two weeks later, he came back and asked if he could rejoin the class. He said there were too many gang members at the high school and that trouble would be easy to fall into.

Again, without the school at El Santo Niño, without a place to go and make contact with an adult community that had a direction for him, he would have lost what he had gained after only a short time back in the old environment—like people who regain weight if they leave their diet programs without transition periods.

I enjoyed having him back, because I had missed him. Later that year, my brother and several friends organized a mountain religious retreat that most of the gang attended, along with the kids at St. Vincent's. It was strange retreat, a lot of highs and lows; and on Saturday night, after affirmations and confessions, two of the gang kids went off and broke windows, turned over beds, and went a little nuts. Silent, in town for Christmas, started it—as I knew he might. I was not ready for him, my gut told me to not take him, but I did so anyway. He and I discussed this retreat months later and both came to that conclusion.

The next morning, I found that Woody had swept up most of the glass and put things back together. He told me his father had a janitorial service that he helped in, and he knew how to do this quickly. He and I and several members of the team sat around and talked for a while. He was embarrassed for the gang, and it was obvious that he did not consider himself part of their activity. It was also obvious, as we all stood there, that he was making a transition.

By June, his clothing had changed to a kind of shirt and pants that were still khaki-like, but did not look cholo. He hung out with his girlfriend, was helping his father more, had bought a car, and was getting his driver's license that summer by going to summer school. Gang members drive without licenses because they don't go to school enough to take the state-required training course.

Once, while I was teaching, he looked at me and said, "I know what you're trying to do with us," like he knew something the rest didn't. At the end of the school year, and the last time I saw him, he said, "I think I have mainly one thing I can thank you for, and that was the retreat." He didn't tell me what about the retreat he wanted to thank me for. Then he said, "I know only one thing, and that's to work. That's all my father taught me, and that's what I know."

He was now back in the stream, on to a different life. Sharky told me a couple of years later, while he was studying bookkeeping at the Job Corps, that Woody had made a business with his dad and they cleaned factories and buildings downtown, and that he and Lulu had a baby.

None of the other gang members really noticed his departure—it was so gradual, as these things have to be—and they had their own lives to take care of.

"The Best School I Ever Been To"

At report card time, we had our only weapons incident, which consisted of Sleepy waving a gun at my head behind my back. I only found out about it later, after school, when Sad Eyes and Lonely told me. "Arturo, didn't you notice everyone was laughing when you were in the office?"

"Yeah, sort of. Why, what was happening?"

"You can't get mad or we won't say it."

"Okay, what?"

"You know when Sleepy was behind you at the desk? He was waving a gun at your head, pretending he was going to shoot you, 'cause you wouldn't give him his report card."

"God damn. He could have killed me!"

"I know, Arturo," Sad Eyes said, laughing. "But it was pretty funny."

Like I said, that was our only weapons incident. I didn't make much of it.

There's a story behind why I wouldn't give Sleepy his report card. At the beginning of that week, we had all gone to Hollywood to see Luis Valdez's movie, *Zoot Suit*. We were the entire audience during the matinee. Afterward, I asked the students to write me a five-paragraph essay on the points that the movie tried to convey.

121

Sleepy still owed me that paper, and I had told him not to count on getting credit for the year until I received his essay. Apparently, he decided against shooting me in the head and instead wrote a respectable paper. Sleepy even mentioned the symbolism of the beaten Pachuco momentarily transformed into an Aztec warrior and then fading into black.

In my storyteller's mind, that scene in the movie was symbolic for me as well. Our little grant had been spent, and no one had promised new funds. The kids knew I had been trying to raise money and find a new location to continue the school, but by May it was obvious that the effort had failed. At 22, I had the energy to initiate, but lacked the experience to sustain and build. I had known going in this might be the case, and the kids had suspected it as well.

We took a lot of field trips in our last weeks, some educational and others just to enjoy the waning days of our little group. In one of our last excursions, we drove to the Huntington Gardens, which surround a mansion that contains art pieces, books, and famous letters and documents. Tourists visit the museum and then stroll the extensive, cultivated grounds. But since it was late May in Los Angeles, an unexpected light rain sent everyone back to the cars. Happy, Droopy, and Joker asked me to keep walking with them—they wanted to talk to me. I gave my keys to Sad Girl so the students could wait in the van, then set down a trail with the three boys.

We sat on some rocks in the Japanese section of the garden, in a light drizzle, and Happy asked me pointedly, "When are you going to start your life, Homeboy?"

"This is my life," I told him.

"No, Homeboy, a real life. Get married, have money. This ain't shit."

Droopy countered, "No, if he gets married, he won't have time for us."

"Don't be selfish," Joker shot back, looking straight at him as he zipped up his black windbreaker. "We all gotta take care of business." But Droopy was only 14 and of a different perspective from Joker and Happy.

"I hope you guys turn out okay," I said. "I worry about it."

"Where you going?" Joker asked me.

"Compton. I'll be working for a church."

Joker continued, "Does it pay pretty good?"

"No. I might be a priest. I don't know."

Happy teased me over that one. "I knew Homeboy was afraid of that stuff. That's why he never made a *movida** on that lady from USC."

"There you go again," Joker chided me, sounding frustrated. "Man, they got some dangerous hoodlums in Compton. You're gonna get jacked. Can't you go do anything like a normal person?"

"So what's gonna to happen to us?" Droopy asked.

"We have to find new schools for you guys."

But Droopy objected. "I'm not going to go. I'll just get kicked out."

"Just don't be so damn crazy, fool," Joker advised him.

"I can't help it. I'm psycho. Arturo knows how I am. But at Jefferson, I'll kill someone."

Joker brought it back to his own life. "I'm going to Jefferson and finish school, get a job, get married. No more messing around. Take care of my *jefecita*. That's what it's all about."

It was hard to argue with that.

The drizzle had turned to drops, so we started walking back to the van, still talking, but broaching brisker topics: cars, girls, movies, the weekend, getting shot at, finding a job, adventures while drunk. Happy told us that he and Joker got high one evening. "We just started running. I didn't even feel tired. We just ran and ran, all the way into the Harpys' territory, way past the freeway. I felt free, Homeboy."

The rain lightly filtered through the trees overarching the walkway. But the talking stopped when we came to the desert gardens. There were no trees for cover, just every shape of cactus. We booked the last hundred yards back to the van.

---

*   A move.

We spent the last days before the school closed figuring out where everyone was going to end up. Sid Thompson, who oversaw our section of the public school district, made sure our kids got credit for their year at El Santo Niño when they reenrolled in the public school system. Pirate and Playboy decided to continue at a private Catholic school, where one of the priests told me, "We don't kick out, we kick ass." Pirate actually made it onto the basketball team.

We did one more school lesson. Smiley and I went to a laboratory supply store and spent the last of our grant money for 20 preserved fetal pigs for dissection. I just hoped I could avoid a flying pig fight. But the kids were good about the whole thing. We laid the little guys three to a table, and the kids dissected them as I called out steps from a handbook. This capped our investigation into the organs of the body, and school was officially over.

On the last day, everyone got report cards. I gave them all my new phone number in Compton, we talked into the afternoon, and then everyone gradually started off for wherever they were going. Smiley and Sharky hung around. Smiley said he was going to get a car and wanted "to just be able to go to Hollywood and have fun, mess around with girls. Why does there always have to be trouble?"

Smiley left, and Sharky and I talked a bit more. We locked up, made sure we left it clean. The auditorium was empty.

"Doesn't look like our school anymore," he said. "This is the best school I ever been to, Homey."

"Me too. It felt like home here with you guys."

We walked out the side door. I put my arm up, and he leaned into me. There was no one else around, so I put my arm around him as we walked, gave him a strong hug, and kissed his forehead.

"Be careful, all right."

"Don't worry, Homey. I know what's up."

Lessons from the Living and the Dead

The years gradually transformed Happy into a man with high-achieving children, a fine marriage, and steady employment running a warehouse. I had not seen him for 15 years when a reporter for the *L.A. Reader* asked if she could interview some of the students I discussed in the first edition of this book. We went through old addresses and located parents who had stayed in the old neighborhood. This led to a conversation with Happy's mother, who informed me that they had tried to find me for his wedding and that I would be proud of who he had become.

I was proud. Happy offered to host a small reunion for the reporter at his home. I understood that part of the joy of this meeting would be that Happy could present his new house—purchased in the old neighborhood and a great source of satisfaction to him.

"This is my house!" he told me as he patted his heart with his hand. In the bedroom was a computer for his two children, and the little girl was wearing a patch from the ophthalmologist to correct a lazy eye that impeded her reading ability. Both children were in a private school. "They were having problems, getting behind, and I heard that a private school would be better. They have fewer kids there, so we transferred them. What do you think?" I thought I might as well be talking to any middle-class parent out on the West Side, except I was in South Central Los Angeles.

How Happy got here involved hitting the mat a few times, but getting back up for another round. He went though AA and now guards his sobriety with all the care of a good AA participant. His wife stayed with him through the tumbles.

He brought out the homework I used to give him, and he reminded me that I made him read the newspaper before he could pass the year. "Now I read the newspaper every day. I can tell you about Iraq, NAFTA, the elections." As a boy, you would have thought him slow, definitely distracted, and learning disabled in some form. As an adult, Happy displays cleverness, wisdom, humor, and a fast wit that keeps me at attention.

Happy still claims the gang. To him, they and the affiliation they shared are the friends of his youth, they are his memories. They still live in the neighborhood. They have baptized each other's children, gone camping together, grieved for those fallen into homelessness or long-term incarceration, and sometimes buried each other.

Happy would think me crazy if I assumed for a moment that he would participate in a drive-by, commit a criminal act, or be irresponsible as a parent. Like all parents, he thinks this generation is worse, he lectures the local gang members, and he forgets the severity of his own misadventures. Happy understands that the problem was never the gang itself. All kids belong to some kind of group, and the gang was his. The detrimental aspects of his participation were the specific behaviors in which they engaged and which destroyed many of their lives. It is these behaviors he has risen above and overcome.

Other gang members also managed to find proper lives. Playboy became a career officer in the military. Smiley raises British Tumblers, a fine breed of bird, which he sells and enters into competition. Sad Girl, Lonely, and Tiny all finished school and attained varying amounts of higher education. Joker married and has good children and a job he enjoys. He and Happy take their kids camping together. Yogi still works on cars and has a family. Sleepy and Psycho moved out of the neighborhood and have given good accounts of themselves.

Others still struggle.

Sharky, after completing a bookkeeping course, did not find work. The deaths of his older brothers also proved difficult. He does little jobs, attempts to be a good parent to his and Juanita's children, and often has to beg and borrow to get by.

Casper died in 1995. He had recently exited prison. A few days later, while walking to Happy's house to watch a pay-per-view fight, he fell across some young gang members from another neighborhood. They gunned him down. Happy's mother shared with me how, earlier that day, he had been at her house and told her, "I'm glad for Happy. I want to try to put my life together like he did."

Popeye and Pirate struggle with addictions. They live at home, always teetering between making it and bottoming out.

Goofy is dead.

Droopy eventually killed someone and will never leave prison.

Droopy makes me particularly sad. I still picture him learning waltz steps for the *quinceñera*[*] of one of the girls in the neighborhood. I can hear the lecture I gave him for taking my car one day without permission. I can remember his voice saying, "I'm a bad boy," in a slow stupor as Sister Natalia hovered over his silver-coated face. I remember being surprised that he could actually open a remote control, take out the transistors, solder in new ones, and make it work. A little Ritalin, a special school, and some anger management, and he would be out today, and someone else would be alive.

---

[*] A *quinceñera* is a Mexican celebration in which a 15-year-old girl is introduced to society—a coming-out party. The all-day affair involves a special Mass, similar to a wedding, and a choreographed waltz by the teenage escorts at the start of the evening's reception. Quinceñeras can cost thousands of dollars and often place families in considerable debt.

Years after we closed the school, I know what decided the fates of my students: the patient resourcefulness of their parents, schools that either supported or rejected them, and the availability of people who understood how to treat their particular problems and addictions—simple, elusive stuff. If they had the fortune of finding this combination of adults, then a coherent, sustained guidance into adulthood developed for them. A few managed to find it.

Violence is not something you stop by preaching. Violence disappears as children experience success and discipline and begin believing in their own possibilities. While they were members of El Santo Niño, they got back on the track to growing up—they became part of a village with concerned adults preparing children to take a proper place among them. Those students who managed to find this again after the gang school at El Santo Niño closed are alive, sober, and enjoying this day. For those who did not, growing up stopped and they went back to wandering the periphery of this village, struggling for a way back in.

EIGHT STEPS
TO A
GANG-FREE
COMMUNITY

The Gang-Free Community

M y friend Alexis picked me up on a Friday afternoon, and we had lunch at Teresita's, a favorite East Los Angeles eatery. We sat for three hours and talked with many of the locals we know. The owner, Doña Campos, introduced us to a college professor in his early 50s as The Man Who Faced Down Those Cholos.

"It happened so fast," he explained. "I was at the park, and these cholos came up to two young kids and stole their bikes. I ran up to the kids and said, 'Get in the car.' Since the cholos were riding uphill, I caught up with them in a minute. I drove up to them at 50 miles an hour, then screeched to a stop right behind them. They thought they were going to get run over, so they jumped off the bikes and ran into the courtyard of the projects, the Ramona Gardens.

"I told the kids to get their bikes off the ground and stuff them into my Honda. But the two cholitos came back with their homeboys and started rushing me. I grabbed a tire iron out of the trunk and said, 'Come on!' I was pissed off. I remembered what it felt like to be a kid and have my bike stolen, and the adrenaline just gave me a rush.

"The cholo in front put his hand in his shirt and said, 'I've got a gun here.'

" 'Pull it out,' I said. 'Pull it out now and shoot fast, 'cause I'm going to kill you if you don't.' There was a crowd around, but no one called the police. The gang members must have thought I was crazy. They backed off, and I took the kids home with their bikes. I don't think I would do that again, but at the moment, you know... The crazy thing is, I found out one of the gang members was the son of a friend I hadn't seen in years. She called me to apologize."

The story had been the local buzz at the restaurant for the past couple of weeks, Doña Campos informed us. She then sat with us and said, "I go to another church now because the local one has too many of those boys. You never know when the shooting starts. Last week, the son of a neighbor came up to me and said, 'I asked you for a dollar last week and you refused me.' Poor boy, he's a drug addict. Such a beautiful family, but only God knows why these things happen. I told him, 'How could I refuse you a dollar? You know that if you need, and I am able to help, I would never refuse to.' He told me he was the leader of all the local gangs and that he had put the word out that no one was to touch my restaurant. He said I was protected. Poor, crazy boy."

We all knew exactly the kind of boy she was talking about. "That kind of protection is a deal for a dollar," I said. "Maybe you can get it for my dad's Laundramat."

I know that most of the people who read this book are not from areas with gang problems. Many of you are worried or interested in this problem, but it is one you see from afar—on television or in the papers—one which you hope never comes any closer than that. And I know the media portrays these children as an organized army of thugs holding communities hostage.

Not exactly. For those of us who live in these areas, these kids are not simply some evil militia to destroy at all costs. They are our neighbors' sons, our cousins' daughters. They are children we have seen grow up. They sit in the back row at church, they dance at our daughters' 15th *quinceñeras,* and they say hello to us when we pass them by the phone booth at the corner market.

They are children for whom we feel sorry, who die young before us, who stagger the streets drunk or stoned or covered in paint they've been sniffing. They disappear for months or years, come back from jail now and then, and disappear again. We talk over backyard fences about those who died walking down the street, who got shot or beaten, or who overdosed on some drug. We console their mothers and fathers, and we don't know what to do or say to alleviate their parents' shame when one of these children commits a terrible crime.

Nearly all of us as neighbors saw local gang members heading for that life at very young ages; and, like their parents, brothers and sisters, teachers, and neighbors, none of us knew what to do about it. We gave advice, like, "Send them to live in Mexico." Some parents could do this, and it often saved a son or daughter. But no one knew what to do beyond such exile.

Doña Campos told me over lunch, "You must kiss a child, but you must also discipline a child so that he knows where to stand. It takes both." Her children have gone to college. Yet her neighbor also kissed and disciplined and prayed and cried. And, for most of her children, that was enough; yet one staggers the streets asking for a dollar.

For 20 years—sometimes by coincidence, sometimes by compassion—I have found myself working with gang members. Twenty years teaches a person quite a bit. What helps gang members turn it around is no longer a mystery to me. It's pretty ordinary stuff.

When the first edition of this book came out, I spent months traveling, consulting, and helping all kinds of people with their programs to help gang members—everyone from church group sponsors to prison boot camp sergeants. What I learned in that process has made me adamant about a couple of things. I saw success in these programs, but the success lasted only while the gang members stayed in the programs. The boy in the mural project was not out vandalizing while he was in that project; the girl in the rehabilitation home was not taking drugs while living in the home. The boy at juvenile hall became a good student at the jail school, and the kid in the church program worked hard when helping the pastor. What everyone kept asking me was, "How do we make this better? How do we get these kids to really change, so that they're good even when they aren't here?"

The answer is that you don't have to add to any particular program. The community has to put its many great efforts together in a rational manner. At that point, a community may find it has most of the resources to protect, contain, and heal its gang-involved children all day and all year. Sometimes when I say that, people respond, "Well, that's their parents' responsibility," or "Why should we have to put so much effort into these kids? Let them straighten out or rot in jail."

I really have no answer to that, except to say that in the middle of the Arizona desert I saw a people take a much different attitude. Much of this has to do with the fact that on a small American Indian reservation, most people—whether the chief of police or a local gang member—have some relationship to each other, either as a neighbor, cousin, brother, or sister. This makes it very hard to scapegoat anyone. And living on a small piece of desert, where resources are scarce, provides a mentality that nothing should be wasted. This includes children.

On this reservation, the word "community" includes the judges, principals, gang members, pensioners, and police officers. I didn't need to convince anyone that if they all worked together, they could take back their children. In fact, taking that attitude has made everyone's life easier. No one has to do the job alone, and in the long run, an expensive, disturbing problem gets solved.

This community is forming mothers' groups, establishing mentor programs between high-school seniors and freshman at the continuation school, targeting children early and following them, contacting employers about jobs for delinquents, and implementing other wonderful interventions. What is exceptional, however, is that they are coordinating these efforts as a community, with a clear goal of taking back all of their children.

It's a rough road, sure, but the only one that gets us out of this mess without having to leave our children to rot in jail.

In the rest of this book, I offer a series of steps that communities can take that will eliminate the formation of gangs. As you can see, I have a wide perspective on this problem. It is a mental health issue, a child-raising issue, and an educational issue. Certain conditions bring it about, and certain responses bring it to a stop, just like any other human behavior.

The steps I suggest work best if taken in the order I present them here.

Peace.

Step 1:
The Community
Affirms All Its Children

At a powwow on the Pima-Maricopa reservation, I heard something I would someday like to hear in all places that struggle with delinquent children. This particular powwow celebrated a youth conference put on by the youth gang task force. Community parents, children, and leaders all attended in a large circle around the grass arena. Later, gang members, Explorer scouts, parents, beauty pageant contestants, the city manager, and the chief of police would all join in the arena to dance together.

Before the dancing began, the master of ceremonies led the community in an opening prayer. Elected officials, elders, parents, and the whole assembly took part in this blessing:

> We pray for our youth,
> To make them strong,
> Wise, and proud.
> And we pray for those of our youth
> Who sleep tonight behind bars.
> Because we love them also.

It's that last line that I've never heard another community express publicly.

On the Salt River Reservation in Arizona, the Pima-Maricopa Indian Community has a gang problem comparable to that found in many inner cities. Their police force is strained, housing projects struggle, and kids engage in vandalism and violence against each other. This is a new problem for them, and plenty of agony stretches across this small desert nation.

On their side, however, is that fact that the Pima-Maricopa are an ancient and close-knit community. The people know each other well, and kinship is spread across the reservation. Perhaps for that reason, they find it difficult to scapegoat and blame. A young gang member easily is the son of a teacher, who is the cousin of the fire chief and nephew of an elder or minister. School, family, and public institutions are connected by blood and time, such that blame directed at any one of them eventually winds up back in one's own family. The result is an attitude that I don't think exists yet in our American cities, but which must be present for any community that wants to solve its gang crisis.

The Pima-Maricopa accept that they are a community, and community children are everyone's problem. They don't divide children among institutions that never talk to each other. Instead, they sit in a circle, and probation officers, the mayor, tribal elders, school principals, parent representatives, job developers, and mental health directors jointly try to decide what to do. The public institutions, the police, the parents, and the politicians all realize that they have a common concern that requires all of their cooperation and common sense.

They understand that "bad" children are no less a part of their community than the "good" children. They see the need to put as much effort into the successes of their prodigal sons and daughters as they do toward the successes of those children who have met expectations. Gang members are, first, community children to be fostered, not invading armies to be fought off.

I have one memory of my time with the Pima-Maricopa of which I am particularly fond. It demonstrates the kind of interaction that occurs when a community treats gang members primarily as difficult kids—meaning they are owned and directed, not feared or negotiated with as if they were adults.

I had been brought in as one of the consultants for the community's efforts to reclaim its children. Community leaders conferenced regularly on how to begin fulfilling this mandate, and I had been speaking at one such gathering. Seated against the walls were citizens of the community, including teenagers, who had come to listen and take part in the conversation. Normal questions followed about details, program costs, and logistics.

Directly facing me, at the back of the room, a teenager stood up and raised his hand. He was a tall, thin gang member, about 17 years old. "This is all good," he declared, "but you can't do anything for us unless we want you to." The challenge had been made, and I realized this would be an interaction that would either hearten or discourage the community's efforts. I had just made a speech about how we could change the forces alienating our children, and this young man had called me on it.

I have been a family therapist for many years, and such comments are to be expected from teenagers. In time, one learns to welcome them. As in family therapy, the gang member spoke from the midst of a people who obviously loved him and among whom he felt safe. I responded as I would have in my own office:

"Thank you. You're a teenager, and I think I would have no respect for you if you didn't rebel, at least a little, against this massive adult effort. That's your job as a teen. But our job as adults is to take care of you, to keep you safe, and to make sure you get the best. And it's our job whether or not you agree to that. That's what adults are for. You keep voicing your thoughts. But we will fail as adults if we think we need our children's permission to do what's right for them. You don't have to like what we come up with, but you will have to live with it. If we are afraid of our own kids, we're not going to get very far in this community."

The young Pima gang member did exactly what I had seen teens do over and over in therapy: He gave me a hard look, and then a small smile. Teenagers start a lot of fights that they want us to win. They'll just never admit that in words.

The beginning, the first step, in solving the gang problem, comes when a community publicly decides to reown all of its children, when its leaders are not afraid to publicly announce about those behind bars that "we love them also." As a community stops fearing its own children and instead begins to plan for them, the battle turns in its favor.

Step 2:
The Children's Advocate and the Child-Raising Community

Promises are easily forgotten. Intentions often result in little more than endless talk at town meetings. Productive conversations depend on agreement about specifics. The "gang problem" is not specific enough. You are not fighting gangs. A community that decides it is going to wage war on 14-year-olds has forgotten who the adults are in this mess.

The real fight involves the community's hesitation at admitting that certain children need more and different kinds of help and figuring out how to provide that help. To win that fight, the productive one, you need information. You need the specifics that explain how the gang-involved children in your child-raising community fare in areas critical to healthy youth.

A town meeting must begin with every citizen obtaining lists describing the reading levels of gang members in their community, the numbers in juvenile hall, the unemployment rate among gang members, their levels of addictions, services available to gang members, their levels of participation in organized recreation, and the number of gang members with access to support groups and therapeutic services. Now you have something specific to talk about and something to solve.

A community needs to get the numbers, set goals around those numbers, and then hire someone to keep track of progress. The person who does this job keeps the community honest and working. I call this person the children's advocate, because by continuously reminding a community about its promise and keeping the specifics before the community, they keep the "bad" children from being forgotten. A children's advocate will, at minimum, do this for your community. Such a person will provide the numbers that allow your community to talk, think, and plan.

What exactly is a child-raising community? In terms of the gang problem, it contains one high school and the junior high and elementary schools that feed into it. This comprises the group of adults who take a child from birth and jointly raise him or her to adulthood. This group of parents, teachers, police officers, business people, recreation directors, psychologists, ministers, and politicians is the village that raises children. It is not necessarily a geographic community: Teachers and other adults who work with kids sometimes live in other parts of town, for example, and kids are often bused to schools in other communities. But to solve the gang problem, these are the people who must call each other family.

The citizens of such a community should be able to pick up a local newspaper and find out how many of their community's children are in juvenile hall, how many are learning disabled and receiving services, and how many failed English in the local high school. A children's advocate gathers such information and makes sure it gets to the public on a regular basis. This allows the entire community to know how it is doing and what needs more attention. You would be amazed at how much more effective a community becomes when it has real information to work with.

How many of your neighborhood children read at grade level? How many are in juvenile hall this month? Are the numbers worse or better than last year? How many of those in gangs need help with addictions? Is this help available? Does your community need a reading center? For how many children? Are there enough uniforms and sufficient transportation, for sixth graders who want to play soccer and whom teachers think are at risk for gang involvement? How many tutors would it take to get every sixth grader into junior high with a literacy rate that would ensure they can understand their textbooks? How many mentors would be needed to serve every junior high student on probation?

You need the numbers.

Once a community accustoms itself to hearing these statistics regularly, then it becomes aware of its children in the same manner that it is aware of the record of its local sports franchise. This is happening already in terms of some school-wide test scores that are published yearly. As you've noticed, now that these test scores are available, politicians, researchers, educators, and voters take them very seriously.

Keeping track of our "bad children" makes them visible and real to us as children. And gathering this information as a community forces us to think of ourselves as people with a common cause—as a family, a clan, a village, or one big company—as a group of people who must put their heads together and figure out what to do with all of its children.

A children's advocate calls our attention back to the problem and argues on behalf of the bad apples. No one does that now—no one lobbies for the special needs of gang-involved children. Someone in the community has to make this his or her job, or we simply won't get around to those kids, and promises we make in community meetings will end up being broken.

Step 3:
Creating and Supporting
Transformative Schools

Several years ago, I participated in a version of the Scared Straight program. In this particular case, I went with the students from one of the local high schools. On this special day, the top Latino students toured a local university to motivate them toward college. The troublesome students toured the local youth camp, one of the places to which juveniles are sentenced, the idea being that this would motivate them away from delinquency.

The show delivered. Students marched through corridors and listened to screaming inmates; they looked in tiny cells with exposed toilets. One girl behind a metal door gave a haunted-house shriek and cried for the passing students to come join her. Then the inmates gave presentations.

The first, a huge Mexican boy, looked at our males and asked, "Are you from Santa Barbara?" They answered by nodding slightly. "Good. The last boy from Santa Barbara turned into my toy. I'll be waiting for you." Another inmate described the toilet situation and told the group that here their humanity would be lost. They would have no privacy, wipe themselves in front of other prisoners, never be able to do one thing without permission and observers. A young woman talked about missing her friends and mother and how she wished she could do it all over again.

What effect did this have? On the students, no more than a good, scary movie. They talked about it at McDonald's in the same excited voices they would use if they had attended a gory slasher film. It was theater, and they knew it. But that's not the point.

The tour did have a powerful positive effect, but not on those students it was intended to impress. The real value resided in what this project did for the inmate team that produced the program. To be a presenter in this effort, juvenile inmates had to show exemplary behavior and be role models to other inmates. They had to memorize their scripts and go over them critically with the officer in charge of the program. After each presentation, the officer and the other volunteers rated their delivery, gave advice, and offered congratulations.

This program involved a lot of extra work for these incarcerated volunteers, yet they received nothing in return. Absolutely nothing. They did not get time off their sentences, extra goodies, money, or a chance to go home. Nothing. Instead, they were actually scrutinized closer than other inmates and punished more severely for infractions. But they loved the program, and they loved the officer in charge.

For these incarcerated youth, the opportunity to be special, to accomplish something, to have a coach and mentor, to be part of a winning team meant everything. It also provided a structure, supportive peers, skills, a caring mentor, recognition and reprimands, and continuous feedback. It provided all of these daily, and right where the kids lived. Combined with the regular schooling provided at the youth authority, the addition of this program gave these adolescents the training, support, and direction they needed as kids becoming adults.

The youth authority camp was not having this powerful impact on the other delinquents. The other juveniles did not experience the attentive eye of an adult with a plan for them, they did not have a peer group that felt like a team, and their victories were not celebrated.

Just as the first step is for a community to see these children, so the second must be to support and create places that provide the daily education, mentoring, direction, encouragement, and help that these kids require. This community place must be where the kids belong, it must be close to home and part of the neighborhood, and it must be a place with a plan. For the Scared Straight inmate team, they found a place with a plan inside of the youth camp.

But what happens back in the neighborhood? Who takes the torch? Where do these teens go to control their addictions, get support and references when applying for their first jobs, learn to read, have hyperactivity or a learning disabilities diagnosed, or find athletic teams to participate in? These inmates are still teenagers; they have miles to go, and unless the local community has a plan for them, they won't make it.

"Bad Kid" Schools

Once a community has taken a vow to acknowledge, support, and keep track of all its children, including the "bad ones," then it must acknowledge, support, and keep a keen eye on the places where these "bad kids" will be served and transformed. Gang schools, opportunity rooms, or wherever else a child-raising community decides to gather its wayward children, must be at the center of the community's attention if the gang problems are to go away.

I know it irks people to celebrate the accomplishments of "bad kids." Read the Bible and the story of the prodigal son. The "good kids" will do well in this world. They receive our praise, our trophies, our financial aid packages, our trust, and our jobs; everything we have is theirs. But the "bad kids" come home to us with nothing, and we have to let them know that they count. We have to let them know that we are glad they are home. This means a few fireworks and a little extra attention.

We do want to solve this problem, right? Then we need to provide "bad kid" schools with

- small student-teacher ratios, with well-trained aides;

- ties to the business community to provide each delinquent a chance to learn how to apply and interview for jobs and how to work;

- weekly support groups—led by teachers, probation officers, or counseling interns from local colleges—aimed at meeting individual goals, such as sobriety, attendance, getting to work on time, and not breaking probation;

- ties to cultural and athletic opportunities, both with local high schools and with recreation centers and other sponsors;

- visits from local court judges who sentence these youths, to encourage them and let them know that everyone is working together to keep them on track;

- parent support groups;

- field trips to colleges, junior colleges, training centers, and other places that we want to make familiar so students feel at ease visualizing themselves attending there;

- access to specialists who can diagnose learning problems and emotional difficulties and suggest remedies and resources;

- well-publicized rituals and ceremonies marking the small, but important accomplishments of these students. A newspaper group photograph, a certificate, a good word to a parent could all acknowledge such accomplishments as attending class 80% of the time, meeting important academic goals like reading improvement, maintaining sobriety for a certain number of months, not breaking probation, or obtaining a job and keeping it. Each brick counts. Celebrate so that it sets well.

There are many examples of schools that currently try to do this, and they succeed with little funding and scarce attention. I am familiar with the Soledad Enriched Action Schools of East Los Angeles, The Expeditionary Schools of Santa Barbara County, and the Desert Eagle Charter School on the Salt River Reservation. There are probably hundreds that I don't know about. The impediment is not that these schools are rare; the problem is that they are invisible and seen as peripheral to the job of educating a community's youth.

The small "bad kid" schools that most school districts sponsor don't have football teams or booster clubs. They are seen as transitory places. This is wrong. They must be schools that are alternatives for kids—many, many kids—who need the intimate structure of such schools to succeed. We need to be as aware of what these schools do and the resources that they need as we are of our regular secondary schools.

All of this takes money, but not much more than we already spend. The most significant difference will be that, instead of these schools being invisible and without much respect, they will become sources of attention and pride in their communities.

In your community, how many kids need this kind of a school? What does your local "bad kid" school need to educate every gang member on probation, every gang member who is feeling defeated in regular school? What do they need to successfully make every such student a confident, competent adult?

Imagine if they succeed in this task.

Step 4: Parents as Partners, Not Patients

In Ventura County, California, one of the public schools decided to put together a program for the parents of gang-involved students. This turned out to be a weekly event in which parents received instruction on better parenting strategies. To her surprise, the coordinator found that the parents of gang members differed substantially from each other. It became difficult to know what to teach them. Some needed basic ideas about parenting, while others could have taught the coordinator some lessons on the subject. There was no stereotypical "gang parent" to target and fix.

The program proved very helpful, however, to parents in a way the school hadn't envisioned. After the program, parents began having frequent conversations with each other that went something like this:

"Are you Shorty's mother? My son says he was at your house last night."

"No, the boys didn't come over. I don't know where they were."

And then a third mother would overhear and offer, "They came by my house with beers and then went to a party on 32nd Street. They said. . . ."

151

Eventually, the mothers exchanged phone numbers and agreed to call each other when in doubt about their children's whereabouts. These conversations also helped locate whose house was being used for ditching parties during the day. Soon, certain mothers who were home during the day made it a habit to check other homes to find out if the kids were sneaking out of school and partying.

The Soledad Enriched Action School in East Los Angeles organizes mothers into a phone tree. They call each other if any of them hear of fights or other trouble. This allows mothers to call police, keep their children' home, and intervene in other appropriate ways.

The key to using parents is seeing them as partners, not patients. If we are going to solve the gang problem, we must stop scapegoating parents and start consulting them. I travel to communities all over the country that are trying to develop programs for helping delinquents. At meetings, I see police officers, teachers, psychologists, activists, ministers, and even gang members. But I never see the parents of gang members. Surely, if they can round up gang members, they can also invite their parents. But no one does this. They prefer talking to the kids and asking them to solve problems, rather than talking adult-to-adult and coming up with coordinated strategies to get the kids in check. That has to stop.

It's easy to talk to a gang member. The gang member is a kid and is going to tell you how horrible his or her parents are and that you never want to talk to them. The gang member is never going to say, "Yes, my parents are worried about me, and you all should get together with them and figure out how to help me and keep me in line." What teenager has ever uttered those words? No, a teenager wants to keep you as far away from his or her parents as possible. Communities that buy into that fall into a very dysfunctional pattern.

You don't solve the gang problem by talking to gang members. You solve it by getting the adults together—teachers, judges, probation officers, civic leaders, and parents—and deciding how to help, direct, and properly raise some very difficult children. If the conversation among these parties is honest and nonblaming (a good mediator helps), then everyone will have advice to offer, insights to contribute, and areas in which they feel they could use some help. I assure you, everyone in this picture can use some help.

One of the interactions I most frequently experience in visits to communities is an encounter with a parent who pulls me aside after a meeting and desperately wants to talk to me. In a rough *barrio** of El Paso, one such parent was an important local minister. After a community meeting, he met me by the punch bowl and, in a very pained voice, told me, "I have almost killed some of my boy's friends. I told them if they come around here, I'll shoot them. My blood pressure isn't good. I'm just so angry. I'm a minister, people look at my family, and I can't even control my own boy."

I asked him, "Is he doing drugs, missing school, or getting arrested?"

"Not yet. He's not that kind of boy. But he wants to be tough, and he just has become disobedient and full of attitude. I think he's more of a wannabe, but it's driving us crazy."

After more punch-bowl talk, it became apparent that this minister really needed to talk to other parents in his same situation. This good man and his wife were living with shame, fear, worry, and anger. They had no one with whom to share this and whom they felt would not condemn them. They also had much to offer. Their parenting skills appeared fine by the looks of their other children, and as clergy, this man could be an example to others that even ministers struggle with their children—something in which other parents in a support group could take great comfort.

What would most benefit this man, and most parents of gang-involved children, would be contact with other parents with whom they could share the burden and from whom they

---

*   Neighborhood.

could take a bit of encouragement. What would most benefit community leaders would be to have the parents of gang members involved as respected partners—not disregarded as scapegoats—in this difficult task of raising children in hard environments.

Step 5:
Supporting Transitions
Between Institutions

A few years ago, the probation department referred a 15-year-old gang member for counseling at a clinic I managed. Guillermo had been arrested for the first time, and this occasioned the referral as part of a diversion program.

The boy's parents were older and had a strange and time-consuming burden. Their oldest son, who had just turned 20, had experienced a sudden onset of schizophrenia his senior year of high school. He now required therapy, medication, and vigilance. The oldest daughter was in her mid-20s and autistic. She sat in the living room, unaware of her surroundings, and required help in basic tasks.

Unlike most gang members, Guillermo had a rather ordinary experience in the primary grades, with only minor academic difficulties. After his older brother's change, however, he became distracted in the classroom—understandably, as his home life became chaotic, his parents became challenged for time to spend with him, and he began to feel guilt about his brother's condition. In the seventh grade, Guillermo's behavior worsened. He progressed into a chronic truant, became a discipline problem in the classroom, and befriended gang members to hang out with when not in school.

But someone at Guillermo's junior high had a thinking cap on. Beginning in the eighth grade, a mentor assigned to him began making sure he attended classes and completed assignments daily. This intervention improved his attendance remarkably. The real genius of the plan, however, occurred when the junior high school held its end-of-the-semester assembly. Standing before the whole school, the principal asked Guillermo to come forward from his seat. When he arrived at the podium, the principal honored him as the most-improved student academically and gave him a special certificate for dramatically improving his attendance. The second semester, he had perfect attendance.

The summer after graduating junior high school, however, a probation officer recommended him for therapy. He had been caught running through the L.A. River bed with another boy. They had a gun and were apparently chasing someone. No one got hurt; no shots were fired; and, since this was a first offense, the judge felt diversion would be the best intervention.

I asked Guillermo about the incident, where he got the gun, and what he had planned.

"My friend got it. Some guy said something to us, and we were chasing him."

"Would you have shot him?"

"I don't know. Maybe. We were just running. I don't know what I'm doing. I know I'm going to mess up from now on."

In therapy, he often referred back to the assembly where he had been honored. Even several months later, the memory of being applauded before all his peers gave him a strong shot of pride. But he felt scared now, and he started to sabotage himself. I think he actually looked to the emotional safety of a juvenile hall school.

"I'm going to get lost," he said when he talked about entering high school in the fall. "I don't think I can keep myself working there [when he would enter high school in the fall]. I just don't think so."

The recognition, the mentor, the principal's acknowledgment, all of these had given him a sense of belonging to the school and the motivation to be his best self. But going to high school terrified him, in the way an alcoholic dreads being in a bar. He felt he would be alone there, unknown, and without the support that had given him the courage to change his habits.

Sure enough, he fought another student within two weeks of the semester's start and received a three-day suspension. Guillermo told me that the halls were packed so tight he couldn't breathe, that courses moved too quickly. In a word, he panicked.

Fortunately for Guillermo, the new school cooperated once I called them and gave them some background. They asked him to try out for basketball, and the coach made a point of befriending him; one of the counselors decided to make a personal effort to become Guillermo's mentor for the year. His parents kept bringing him to therapy even after the diversion program stopped paying.

Guillermo proved luckier than other boys. A supported transition from one institution to another patched itself together long enough to get him set and succeeding again. But it was really just luck. The institution itself had no mechanism for this, and it just happened that some good people decided to take it upon themselves. Because of that luck, the good work at the junior high did not get lost, and the support by the high school made it possible for him to readjust and get back his motivation and nerve.

I am sure, however, that there were quite a few other Guillermos at that school for whom these things did not happen.

After El Santo Niño closed, I kept up with some of the students, especially the ones I worried about. I took Sharky out to lunch that September to see how he had been holding up in public school. I told him that I had asked administrators to look after him.

"I know, Homey," he said, his face a bit serious and looking to the side. "I can feel, like, people, teachers, know what I'm doing." He enjoyed this sense of importance, and it made him optimistic about doing well. The surveillance he felt soon ended, however. It really consisted of one administrator taking a bit of time out every week to see him for a few minutes. But the administrator had 3,000 other teens to care for, and this ritual diminished in frequency until it disappeared.

Sharky had serious reading disabilities, an addiction to glue, and years of failure behind him. Although he had progressed significantly in reading and had gained considerable academic knowledge, this had occurred within a very controlled and safe setting. Going from El Santo Niño, a one-room schoolhouse with 30 friends and an empathetic staff, to a junior high with 3,000 students, seven periods a day, and a strange, year-round schedule, simply overwhelmed him. He got thrown in the deep end without anyone to swim beside him for a few laps.

Without the handrail of supportive adults, he faltered. Unlike Guillermo, no therapist made phone calls for Sharky, no counselor found time to monitor him, and no one volunteered to get him involved in special activities at school. He had nothing to hold onto, so the transition from one institution to the next slipped into failure. Within two months, he had dropped out. Sharky drifted for several years until being placed in the Job Corps by a probation officer.

I compare this story with my friend Jacob's experience with his daughter. His oldest children went through puberty un-scathed, but the youngest daughter has had a tumultuous adolescence.

Jacob sent his daughter to therapy, then drug rehabilitation, then family counseling, and to various private schools. They went through tough love, and still she declined into greater drug use, running away, and continuous disregard for parental cur-fews. Jacob's bright daughter did well in school when she wanted to, and found work easily when she tried.

"You don't know what it's like to see your daughter stoned all the time, completely unavailable to you," he told me wearily. "I hate wondering where she is, if she's coming back tonight or tomorrow."

After a final round of rehab and ultimatums, Jacob decided he would do anything to help her. He didn't want to turn her loose, as the tough love approach required, so he found a program in another state. It cost $21,000 for six months. Jacob put up $7,000; his ex-wife, another $7,000; and the grandparents mortgaged a house for the final $7,000.

The intervention worked. Not only did Jacob's daughter not relapse into old behaviors upon leaving the program, but she became a youth mentor to other girls and has gone on successfully to college.

To help one girl with an addiction took $21,000, countless hours of therapy, special schools, parent seminars, and continuing peer support groups. Everyone I have talked to in the middle class finds this unsurprising, and many have stories of family or neighbors who have invested similarly in troubled teenagers. That being the case, how do we expect an addicted teen—with problems compounded by learning disabilities, school failure, poverty, and other difficulties—to transition into public school from incarceration, in the middle of the year, and hit the ground running? How do we expect a troubled sixth grader to enter a junior high school and not get lost? How do we expect a boy or girl to leave a group home after a two-month recovery program and go back to his or her neighborhood without any support and think that he or she will do well?

One constant about gang members is that they shuttle between institutions—juvenile hall, to youth camp, to group home, to special school, to regular school, then back to juvenile hall, and so on. The reason they move so much is that they fail; they mess up; they stop showing up; and, in the end, a probation officer or judge has to find another placement for them. If we can get them started well, however, the likelihood of negative experiences diminishes greatly.

All child-raising communities—and here, children's advocates could streamline the process—need to create mechanisms in their schools that allow gang members to get good starts upon entry. Some ideas:

- Establish liaisons at high schools and junior high schools who visit inmates at juvenile hall. These liaisons let incarcerated students know they are not forgotten and also prepare for their return by informing teachers, contacting mentors, and arranging for welcoming orientations.

- Establish a mentor program for students on probation.

- Have a special aide or volunteer check in during each class to verify attendance, observe behavior, and collect reports from teachers. The information gathered from observation and teacher input can be used to determine what supports students will need to keep up, or if students need a continuation school, fewer classes, or different classes.

- Create an ongoing support group for students on probation that meets during school hours.

- Create a system of ceremonies and rewards at the school for returning students—for example, after two months of good attendance, a special lunch. At the end of a semester, arrange for acceptance into a school-community business program that supports after-school jobs for teens on probation.

- Save the last period for a special class in which students present teacher signatures confirming that they have completed the day's work in each period. This class should also have several volunteer college students as aides who can help with homework assignments that can be completed at this time.

- Require participation in a school activity or sport, and assign a mentor to encourage students in this endeavor. Such activities promote contact with new peer groups for gang members.

As I complete this book, I am a counselor at one of the finest urban public schools in California. Yet even here, with an excellent administration and fine staff, there is no one to do all these things. In fact, as we aggressively pursue higher standards, wayward kids become harder to serve and maybe less welcome in our regular programs.

Yet a little awareness goes a long way.

Several of the students I counsel are on probation and have come to my attention as they enter our school after months in various forms of detention. José played football one semester but was expelled after he tried to break into a car with friends. His last years of school have been chaotic as he bounced between schools and juvenile detention. When he arrived at our school, his mother and sister both said they would be available for any kind of help I needed. José knows how to weld and do construction from working with his father. He is bright, yet does poorly in school. He also has a temper and an attitude that prefers failure to backing down.

I asked José to check in every morning and before leaving every day. I worked out classes that he could handle, with a morning study period he could be late to, and with a teacher who was willing to mentor him. He immediately began doing better. At the end of the semester, he had a B average. I brought this to the attention of the principal, who congratulated him in person. It was a small gesture, but large in his life.

The interesting thing is that even after he no longer had to check in with me officially, he still did. There he was every morning and before going home. If I got too busy to take notice of his progress, he began to miss classes. This was a bright kid who, for reasons of his own, needed much more attention and encouragement than most kids his age. When he received it, he did well. There are lots of kids in juvenile hall just like him.

Three weeks ago, a girl came in from juvenile hall and told me, "I don't belong here. I haven't been in a regular school since I was 12 years old. I don't know a thing about school." She had been arrested at 12 and had spent the last couple of years moving around the system. I gave her a pep talk, got her into selective classes, found her a service position in an office with a secretary with whom she could bond, set her up for tutoring, and told her to check with me twice a week. So far it looks good.

As a guidance counselor, however, I have nearly 800 students, all of them deserving of my attention. This kind of intense attention for one student is not the job of the guidance counselor. It is really no one's job to do all this. And that's what has to change if we are serious about the gang problem in our communities.

There is a convention in psychology that says the best way to predict what someone will do in the future is to see what that person has done in the past. Another defines insanity as doing the same thing over and over but expecting a different result each time.

I have been describing kids who have failed consistently and who will probably fail again. If we are to be successful with these kids, who come to us regularly from the juvenile justice system, we must have people who are designated to shepherd them along and who can make sure something different happens this time around.

Isn't this obvious?

Step 6:
Identifying Disabilities

I teach a psychology course at East Los Angeles City College. Many of my students are teacher's aides (TAs) in the local elementary schools. One of these, a very bright and motivated young man named Sergio, approached me one day after class. "I have this 7-year-old I think is like the kids you were telling us about."

"What does he do, Sergio?"

"Nothing. He won't work unless I'm sitting by him. The moment I leave he just sits."

"How much does he remember at the end of the day?"

"I don't think he remembers anything. When the teacher asks a question, he just answers with part of the question, but it doesn't make any sense."

"Has he been tested or referred to anybody?"

"No."

"Why don't you ask the teacher to do this?"

"I'm just a TA. I don't know if she would appreciate me telling her what to do."

"Does she think he has a problem?"

"She has a lot of students. I don't know."

"If you're afraid it's inappropriate to say anything, I'll show you how to teach this student, but it's going to take a lot of patience. Teach this student as a personal project, and it will teach you something as well about working with disabled children."

The Making of a Gang Member

No one description applies to every person in a youth gang. But most share a recurrent problem. Most have difficulty in school, and at least half of them, when tested, have learning disabilities. *At least half.* Many studies find much higher numbers than this. Apparently, we have something to deal with here, and if it could impact half of our delinquents, that would facilitate a dramatic reduction in the scope of our gang problem.

Let me explain, from my experience of following kids in school for the last 20 years, how many kids become gang members.

You begin with a child who, in kindergarten, has trouble with the names of colors, letters, and figures. In first grade, he has difficulty remembering numbers and syllables, and he falls into the lowest reading group or becomes the least able member of a cooperative, mixed group. The effect is the same. The child might be a slow learner, or he might be an average or even bright student, yet he appears spacey, impulsive, introverted, disorderly, hyperactive, angry, or bored. The reasons are many, but the result is the same: He doesn't keep up with the others.

Sometimes this child is held back, but usually not. Either way makes no difference. Second grade goes similarly, and by the third grade, the child is significantly behind the other students. This is a critical year, because it is here that kids go from basal reading ("See Juanito run.") to content reading in academic areas.

The parents get called to meetings. In the early grades, teachers give suggestions, depending on the experience of both the teachers and parents, on how to help. These usually don't help much, and the parents begin to get frustrated and to frustrate the child. In the later grades, these meetings become mostly nagging sessions in which the parents are told to keep the child in line, make him do his homework, and so forth. If the parents try hard to enforce the teachers' desires, then home also becomes a punitive place for the child.

The student begins to struggle with academic subjects. Historical information, geography, science facts, these mostly go by him. Very little seems to stick or to be meaningful. The texts are cryptic to him, tests are dreaded, and reading aloud is embarrassing.

The youngster begins to learn how to hide and how to distract the teacher and the class. He either bullies or disappears. The teacher isn't sure what to do. She tries not to embarrass the child, to give some work he can do; usually, this means dittos, fill-in-the-blanks, or cooperative group work where the kid can do some task for the group but in reality is learning very little. The student learns to follow a direction, how to fill up space. When I ask this kind of student what he did in school today, he answers, "We did work."

"What kind of work? What did you learn?"

"We did work, school work."

By fourth grade, the child begins to get a little bolder in his dissent. He might attempt to mimic gang attire if his parents are not wise to it. The student is now a problem in the class and has usually formed friendships with other such "problem children," both in class and on his block. Other children are aware of him and know he doesn't do his work, can't read, doesn't know his multiplication tables, and is always in trouble. The kid internalizes this description of himself easily, since he lives it daily.

Some schools try to shield kids from this by eliminating grades or using cooperative groups where individuals aren't tested. Some schools mainstream, others separate. None of this makes a difference, as kids will compare themselves anyway. Child psychologist Erik Erikson (1968) tells us that the elementary school age is the age of "competence," and children are constantly competing to see who measures up. They don't fool themselves. If a kid can't keep up, all the others know it, and he knows they know it, no matter how teachers may try to hide it. The importance of this cannot be minimized. A teacher may speak of every child having worth. What the kid perceives is,

"Everyone else can do things I can't. Everyone else receives awards I never get, no matter what I do."

As the fifth and sixth grades come upon him, he has now experienced several years of school as a place of failure, a place where he just gets through the day, a place where he is last in everything. He has learned to hide well or to get attention through mischief. He is used to the parent meetings and the principal's office and doesn't fear them much. A feeling of "me versus them" forms within him.

Puberty kicks in with its self-consciousness, and this makes his situation more apparent, more felt. Up to now, he has taken failure as children do: They feel its sting, but the world is still small, and adults take care of the its business while you play. But as adolescence approaches, the need to have a place for oneself, a group of friends, an identity separate from others and from adults, begins to push at the child.

What this kid knows is that he is not one of the competent people, that school is painful and shameful, and that he is not a "good boy" to the adult world outside his home. Even at home, where he may be helpful and still a decent son, parents struggle to understand and deal with his growing rebellion and inability to act in school like "good" children do.

Seventh grade comes around, and the kid is moved to a huge school with hundreds or thousands of other students, and with many teachers. If he was struggling before, he is now completely lost. He quickly gravitates to others like himself—others who can't stand class, who can't read the books, and who live from threat to threat from parents and teachers and every adult they know to please behave and please try.

Teachers in our student's junior high school have 30 or 40 pupils per class. They must teach children who read from a second-grade level to above average, plan several lessons a day, and correct a load of papers each evening. Teachers immediately spot our student as one of the hyperactive, sullen, angry, unmotivated, or unprepared. They find it difficult to either contain or motivate this kind of student on a daily basis. For the good of the class, this child spends a lot of time in detention, writing standards, or just sitting in his seat doing nothing, but at least being quiet under threat of punishment. This kid will seldom turn in homework or complete assignments, and the teacher feels she can do nothing to force him.

Our student quickly discovers by accident, and by tutelage from older friends, that in this big school, nothing happens if you don't go to class. He figures out the system: In only one of the six periods does the attendance office count to see if the student is at school. He shows up only for that class. He intercepts notes and phone calls from teachers and administrators. He hides report cards, forges signatures, and changes grades or lies to parents about their meaning. He quickly discovers that a teacher with six different classes, a homeroom, and 150 teenagers to deal with doesn't have time to call his home if he isn't in class or hasn't completed an assignment. The easiest trick he learns involves giving the wrong phone number when filling out registration forms. This simple maneuver frustrates the first few attempts to contact his parents.

Eventually, someone does find our escape artist. They call or visit his home and arrange a meeting with his parents. The teacher nags the parents, who nag the child. Eventually, too, the parents stop showing up for these meetings, but not before having made the child aware that he is a source of shame to the home, so that the street is now the only place with any source of reward.

Our student occasionally attends a class, and the teacher hates it. It creates another dilemma for a teacher who is already struggling to make the class work for the students who attend regularly. Now there is this kid who has no clue what's going on and no book, pencil, or paper. The kids makes a fuss if ignored, yet the teacher only hopes he doesn't create a problem, and searches for some way to keep him busy. At all inner-city schools I taught in, teachers looked forward to the passing weeks, as these students would eventually stop coming altogether, and then the teacher could relax with a smaller, more consistent class. This sounds negligent, but in their shoes, you would feel the same way.

Our teenager joins with other teens like himself, and they begin to spend most of their time at the local park, at a house where they have ditching parties, in an abandoned building, in arcades. They roam the streets and get high with cheap drugs like beer, paint, glue, and marijuana. As they wander around neighborhoods, it becomes routine to pilfer things, climb in open windows, take a stereo from a car, or go for joyrides. Occasionally, they'll meet up with boys from another neighborhood and have a scuffle. Why? Because claiming a park or street and fighting for it is a source of accomplishment to kids who have no other trophy to put on their mantles. And when you are 14 and not feeling very good about yourself, it's easy to be self-destructive.

If there was no gang in the neighborhood before, they have formed one now. If this neighborhood and its schools have a history of generating children who fail, then there will be many friends to find on the street, and these friends will have a history as the local gang.

Sometime in junior high, this youth will get caught and spend a few weeks or months in juvenile hall or some special detention camp. Here, he will run into other gang members, students that went to his same elementary school, old acquaintances from his neighborhood. He gets three meals, they make him go to the prison school, and he enjoys it because all the kids are like him and there is discipline here, which he interprets as caring. He sees that it isn't a bad place. And most important, he notices that when he gets released, nothing in his life has changed. Nothing has been lost or gained. This is the fundamental lesson pivotal to an emerging gang life.

He gets a probation officer who sees him once a month and nags him for five minutes, tells him he has to go to school. A judge tells him the same. He tries for a few days and then goes back to what he was doing before. Eventually, he gets caught at something else or for breaking probation and gets sent back to juvenile justice, where a judge gives him a railing about how bad it's going to be from now on. He goes in, gets three meals, works, talks to other gang members, comes out in a few months or a few years, and nothing has changed.

The neighborhood school won't take him back at this point, so they tell him he has to go to a special school or another school, usually further away and across other gang territories. He seldom even tries to attend. The parents are pressured but can't do anything. The kid has developed such a phobia to school at this point that he would rather live on the street or go to jail than go to school.

By the time he is 16, he has a long record of usually petty crimes; of course, some have done much worse. He has not been to school consistently since the sixth grade. The little he learned is forgotten. He has developed addictions and acquired tattoos and social skills—mostly learned in jail—that mark him to any potential employer or school official as a gang member.

Finally, the identity that began to peek at him around the sixth grade is now firmly entrenched, and as he looks at the future, he understands that it will be more of the same. Time on the street, time in jail—a routine. He has no hopes of ever owning a home, earning a driver's license, or having a credit card. These are faraway ideas he associates with that world he was never able to fit into and of which he is now the enemy. He has nothing and believes he will always have nothing. Whatever he makes in occasional profitable thefts or drug sales disappears quickly. There is nothing to lose or gain of any permanence, and so he lives this life on the margin day to day, with little thought of the future. He does not think of consequences, because for his life, there are none that make a difference.

Learning Disabilities and Poverty

A theme throughout this book is that most gang members have histories of difficulty in school, usually from the early grades. Here are a few facts.

The average reading level among kids in juvenile hall is between third and fourth grade. This is true of delinquents in the United States as well as in other English-speaking countries (Berger et al. 1975).

The average rate of learning disabilities in the United States is about 3% of the population, 12% if you include conditions like attention deficit hyperactivity disorder (ADHD). The average rate for juvenile delinquents, however, is 50% for learning disabilities and 90% if you include ADHD and other emotional disorders. That means that 9 out of 10 kids in juvenile hall display some learning or emotional disability. This has been found true in scores of studies conducted on delinquent children (Lorsbach 1992, Morgan 1979, Murphy 1986, O'Connell 1987, Perlmutter 1987, Stanley 1981, Swanstrom 1981, Waldie 1993).

The obvious question is why do so many delinquents have these kinds of disabling conditions? Researchers have uncovered a disturbing phenomenon. If you take 10 babies who are born prematurely, 5 of them from low-income families and 5 from middle-income families, usually all of them will show signs of developmental delays in the first year. Five years later, however, the children from the middle-income families will likely have normal IQs, whereas the children from the low-income families will usually still be delayed. Poverty has adverse affects on the ability of many children in terms of developing their cognitive capacities. This is unfortunate, but true (Beckwith 1984, Begab 1978, Reschly & Jipson 1972, Wilson 1985).

Poverty means poor nutrition, limited health care, and a greater number of prenatal problems. It also means that children are not exposed to learning games, ballet lessons, preschools, and other activities that are available when parents have time, money, materials, and education. Dozens of studies show the benefits of early exposure to learning activities, books, stories, and adult attention in the form of questions, conversations, and play (Jennings & Connors 1989, Kagan 1973, Kagan 1979, McGowan 1984, Roberts 1992, Seki 1985). Such an enriched environment is normative once urban parents have at least middle-income resources, which include such things as education, soccer leagues, health insurance, transportation, and day care, as well as access to children's books and games— all of which are expensive.

Poverty also means that children are not diagnosed early; that problems fester; and that, in overcrowded schools, the psychologists only see the extreme cases. Poverty means that even if parents and teachers know that a child is having difficulty, there are no specialists in the local community who can treat the student.

Most mental retardation and learning disabilities occur among low-income people (Beckwith 1984, Begab 1978, Reschly & Jipson 1972, Wilson 1985).* This is true not only in the United States but in every country that monitors these concerns. This is the reality. The mind, like all other parts of the body, responds to nourishment and stimulation. Time, money, and know-how simply work together in creating environments in which enriched experiences are more likely to occur daily.

But if low-income children are more likely to have intellectual and emotional problems, then why don't they get help in the public schools? Why are they not diagnosed and referred for therapy, vision treatments, medication like Ritalin, and other methods of managing these problems?

Again, the answer lies in time, money, and know-how. It's one thing for a first-grade teacher to have one or two kids who present some difficulties that need testing. A teacher will notice, because the problem children stand out. Since she has only one or two such children in her class, she has time to write the referrals and follow through on the process. The school psychologist, who usually spends only a few hours each week at a particular elementary school, also has time to attend to the referral within a reasonable time frame.

In low-income neighborhood schools, a first-grade teacher may have 5 or 8 or 10 students with difficulties. When a teacher has that many students with problems, however, the students all begin to look normal, and the teacher simply cannot tell when or where she should start the referral process. She knows that the school psychologist will not respond to 10 referrals, and

---

* These studies include rates of retardation among differing economic classes.

the school budget cannot pay for special services for one-third of her classroom.

Because the rate of learning disabilities is only about 3% in the general population, schools are funded with that number in mind. But no one addresses the fact that the rate is much higher in low-income neighborhoods such that most learning disabled kids in low-income areas never receive adequate treatment.

The outcome is that many low-income children with unattended deficits will have difficulty in school, low self-esteem, and high drop-out rates. And kids who have little to lose and who are in need of success and approval will find that approval anyway they can. This might include getting pregnant, becoming adept car thieves, or recognition as the most dangerous, callous kids on this side of the freeway.

Solutions

So what do we do? Unfortunately, nothing that is easy or cheap. The necessary response, if we want to deal with learning disabilities in a way that reduces juvenile delinquency, requires that we plan the following in areas with high gang activity.

This intervention has two parts. First are five considerations necessary for working with individual children who experience learning difficulties of whatever sort. The second set of guidelines are for school districts that wish to adequately deal with large numbers of these children.

For Individual Children with Learning Difficulties

Flexible definitions. There are no exact descriptions of what constitutes a learning disability or how many kinds of learning disabilities exist. Human beings are complicated creatures, and they seldom fit exactly in the boxes we design for them. Legal definitions are necessary for funding, but psychologists know how to work around these. The point is to remain flexible and attend to obvious problems when they present themselves, even if you can't find the exact diagnosis for a child. Use the one that gets closest for the grant, placement, or federal aid, but don't ignore a problem because you cannot label it.

Individualized attention. Regardless of the program in which a child ends up, what matters in the end—and what will prove most effective—is how much individual attention the student receives. Having a high-school senior sit with a slow student and read aloud an hour every day is more effective than hiring a highly paid specialist to work with the student once a week or buying a fancy reading program for the classroom. The more unmotivated, hyperactive, withdrawn, angry, afraid, frustrated, slow, inattentive, or forgetful a child is, the more likely it is that only large helpings of daily individualized attention will make a difference.

Time and pace. Learning and emotional difficulties take years to manage, and nothing can change that fact. You have to plan across years, not weeks, to make a permanent change. In addition, to build a base, a student who is slower or distracted has to master information before moving on. That takes time, and you can only go at the student's speed. No other strategy makes sense.

Priorities and goals. Because students with learning difficulties take longer to master material, need more repetition, and usually have knowledge gaps that must be remedied, you can't throw the entire curriculum at them. Pare it down to what you think will be most beneficial to the students' futures, set goals, and concentrate on meeting them. Setting priorities and establishing goals makes it much easier to coordinate with other institutions to which the student may transfer. A school can inform juvenile hall or a new school about specific academic progress that needs to be continued.

Sharing medical and psychological expertise with parents. Have access to specialists who can prescribe medication such as Ritalin or who know about available therapeutic approaches. Make sure parents are well-informed and that their concerns are attended to, which means follow-up visits and good rapport. Minority parents often tell me that a doctor recommended Ritalin for their child two years ago, but a next-door neighbor said it would be addictive or evil or whatever, so the parents decided to table the doctor's prescription. Parents need someone to talk to, usually more than once, about such concerns.

For School Districts with Large Numbers of Children with Learning Difficulties

Class size should be no more than 20 students throughout elementary school, and no more than 25 in secondary schools. In schools with high numbers of struggling students, the need for special services is significantly reduced when teachers have time to accommodate individual learners.

Flexible curriculum. Free elementary school teachers from curriculum mandates if students are having trouble with basic reading and mathematics.

Elementary classroom aides. Elementary classrooms should have college or high-school student aides who work consistently with small numbers of students.

Secondary classroom aides. Secondary school classrooms should have college-level aides in sufficient numbers to work with kids who need more explanation and encouragement. In choosing to both mainstream and avoid tracking children, we have created classrooms in which one teacher cannot possibly attend to the great variety of students' learning needs. We need more adults in those classes. It may be wishful thinking, but, again, this would work best in a context of 25 students per class.

Special study period. Develop a program that provides something like a study hall, but with a teacher trained in working with kids who have learning difficulties, and with college students to assist as well. This program should be the last period of the day and should be used to settle kids down, motivate them, provide extra explanation, make sure homework is complete and assignments for the evening are neat and noted, and teach other study skills and aids. Of course, this means that a school might have to eliminate a couple of requirements to accommodate this. This does not mean diluting the curriculum, but a school could eliminate one year of physical education and one elective requirement, for example.

Who pays for this? We all do. But we pay anyway if we don't do anything. I would rather have my taxes fund college aides and small classrooms as opposed to jails and more police. Remember, at least half of our gang members are children whom kindergarten teachers could have warned us were heading for trouble. We saw them coming; we knew of the difficulties that would drive them to the streets instead of schools. These are kids who, as teenagers, have little hope for any of the good things that keep most of us working for the future.

Let's keep that in mind, because it is very difficult to punish a kid who feels he or she has nothing to lose.

References

Beckwith, L. (1984, July). Parent interaction with their pre-term infants and later mental development. *Early Child Development and Care, 16* (1–2), 27–40.

Begab, M.J. (1978). The major dilemma of mental retardation: Should we prevent it? *American Journal of Mental Deficiency, 78* (5), 519–529.

Berger, M.; Yule, W.; & Rutter, M. (1975, June). Attainment and adjustment in two geographical areas: II. The prevalence of specific reading retardation. *British Journal of Psychiatry, 126,* 510–519.

Erikson, E. (1968). *Identity, Youth, and Crisis.* New York: W.W. Norton.

Jennings, K., & Connors, R. (1989, June). Mothers' interactional styles and children's competence at three years. *International Journal of Behavior Development, 12* (2), 155–175.

Kagan, J. (1973, November). Cross cultural perspectives on early development. *American Psychologist, 2* (11), 947–961.

Kagan, J. (1979). Issues and evidence in daycare. In W. Michelson & S. Levine (Eds.), *The Child in The City.* Toronto: University of Toronto Press.

Lorsbach, T. (1992, Summer). A comparison of learning disabled and non-learning disabled students on five at-risk factors. *Learning Disability Research and Practice, 7* (3), 137–141.

McGowan, R. (1984, June). The mother-child relationship and other antecedents of childhood intelligence: A cultural analysis. *Child Development, 75* (3), 810–823.

Morgan, D. (1979, Fall). Prevalence and types of handicapping conditions found in juvenile correction facilities: A national survey. *Journal of Special Education, 13* (3), 283–295.

Murphy, D (1986, May–June). The prevalence of handicapping conditions among juvenile delinquents. *Remedial and Special Education, 7* (3), 7–17.

O'Connell, J.C. (1987, September). *A Study of the Special Problems and Needs of American Indians with Handicaps Both On and Off The Reservation, Vol. 2.* Tucson: University of Arizona, Native American Research and Training Center. (ERIC Document Reproduction Service No. ED 294 343).

Perlmutter, B. (1987, April). Delinquency and LD: Evidence for compensatory behaviors and adaptation. *Journal of Youth and Adolescence, 16* (2), 89–95.

Reschly, D.J., & Jipson, F.J. (1972). Ethnicity, geographic locale, age, sex, and urban-rural residence as variables in the prevalence of mild retardation. *Annual Progress in Child Psychiatry and Child Development,* 612–624.

Roberts, R.N. (1992, July–September). "Let momma show you how": Maternal-child interactions and their effects on children's cognitive performance. *Journal of Applied Developmental Psychology, 13* (3) 363–373.

Seki, M. (1985). *Eating Behavior in the Family and the Development of 4- to 5-year-old Children.* Osaka, Japan: Research and Clinical Center for Child Development, 63–71.

Stanley, S. (1981, April.). *The Relationship Between Learning Disabilities and Juvenile Delinquency.* (ERIC Document Reproduction Service No. ED 21 765).

Swanstrom, W. (1981, September). The frequency of learning disabilities: A comparison between juvenile delinquents and a seventh grade population. *Journal of Correctional Education, 32* (3), 29–33.

Waldie, K. (1993, June–July). The relationship between learning disabilities and persisting delinquency. *Journal of Learning Disabilities, 26* (6), 417–423.

Wilson, R.R. (1985, September). Risk and resilience in early mental development. *Developmental Psychology, 21* (5), 795–805.

Step 7:
Something to Care About
and Take Pride In

E d Thrasher wrote a book on gangs in 1927.* It's still one of the best books written on the subject. He took a good, long look at 1,300 gangs in Chicago and came up with some reasonable conclusions.

He observed, among other things, that gang members are a playful, energetic bunch. He also reached an important conclusion about keeping them busy. He said that if you put a gang member in a boxing gym for two hours, then you've kept him off the street for two hours. That's a nice idea. If you give this delinquent a pair of gloves and a trainer and put him in a tournament, however, you have given him a serious hobby and maybe a career. He will now exercise; watch what he eats; get to sleep earlier; and have something to think, talk, and read about. You've now kept him off the streets most of the time. Thrasher knew the importance, even in the 1920s, of developing a teenager's personal interests as a method of reducing delinquency.

Gang members are children. They like to play, they get bored, and they get into mischief when they have nothing to do.

---

*   Thrasher, E. (1927). *The Gang: A Study of 1,313 Gangs in Chicago.* Chicago: University of Chicago Press.

A crucial element in the success I had at El Santo Niño involved finding things for kids to do after school. I tried basketball, soccer, football, boxing, camping, the police Explorers club, speech tournaments, volleyball, car clubs, theater arts, music, bowling, photography, drawing, church groups, and after-school jobs for the older gang members. We even had a movie club. Any interest they showed, or any that I thought they might grow to like, I pushed them into pursuing.

Here's the rub: These kids bring baggage with them. They get frustrated easily, lack discipline, have addictions, compulsively graffiti, have no money, and have intense fears of being shamed before other kids. To successfully introduce these kids to new activities, you have to prepare your expectations. It's the difference between swimming lessons for kids who aren't afraid of the water and swimming lessons for kids who are terrified of the water. It takes a special kind of coach for the second bunch.

If your gang members go to school every day because the school attends to their special learning and emotional needs, that takes care of the day's mischief. And if your gang members are busy in the evening with jobs or hobbies, all under adult supervision, then you've had a whole day without violence or vandalism. Essentially, your community's gang problem has been solved.

So how do you accomplish this? A community must have the following in place to be successful in this endeavor:

- A policy explicitly stating that kids who are on probation, or who have come in contact with the law, must be involved in some structured activity.

- A means of recognizing at-risk children and connecting them to activities. This may have to include expenses such as paying for team uniforms and such.

- A communitywide parent education program about the importance of activities that promote self-esteem and competence.

- Changing school policies so that students in continuation or "bad kid" schools are strongly encouraged and eligible to participate on athletic teams at their communities' regular high schools.

- Developing recreational and artistic activities in detention facilities, and a systematic means of continuing these once kids return to their communities.

Once again, we are talking about gang members as adolescents and planning for them as such. Communities that come together, make these kids visible, and plan for them systematically will regain control of their children. As the guy on the suit commercial says, "I guarantee it."

Step 8:
Promoting Recovery from Addictions

C hemical abuse brings about and exacerbates much of the violence, crime, and personal degeneration among gang-involved youth. I think this is obvious to all of us. The reason I have included this as the final step rather than the first step, however, has to do with what we know about overcoming addictions.

Fortunately, those who work with recovering addicts have developed their field into a mature and useful discipline in recent years. Certificates are now available in chemical abuse counseling, 12-step programs exist in most neighborhoods, support groups are available for all ages, and a variety of rehabilitation programs offer services. The problem at this point is not that we don't know what to do but rather that recovery takes time, continuous support from family (and school, for teenagers), testing, education, and work on strengthening addicts' self-esteem and self-support. For this reason, effective work with addicted gang members will occur only after the community has put into place the previous seven steps in the program I've outlined.

Many gang members are sent to group homes and recovery programs. Many do well while in those programs, but a few months after coming home, old habits begin to resurface. Difficulties at school, failure to find employment, boredom, temptations from friends who still use, and other typical stressors begin to eat away at whatever convictions the gang member has tried to hold onto. As anyone in Alcoholics Anonymous will tell you, no one recovers alone. It takes mentors, meetings, new friends, continuing education, and other methods to sustain recovery.

The pieces are all out there, but they have to be coordinated, and they must follow the gang member from juvenile hall to group home to alternative schools in the community. Support groups must be available at public schools, as well as information and seminars for parents. Recreation programs, employment opportunities, and schools where the youth feels a sense of belonging must be part of an integral recovery program.

Do not be overwhelmed by what I am suggesting. The pieces exist in most communities, and where they do not, a bit of dialogue with local universities, corporations, and government agencies can usually create them. But someone needs to be in charge of this for the community, and someone needs to gather these community resources and coordinate gang members' participation.

Plan carefully. Psychologist Carl Jung believed that when one person attempts to fix another, the first one internalizes the trouble of the latter. The therapist absorbs the anxiety, depression, or despair of the patient. It is easy to do. Jung taught that successful therapy results only if the therapist has an inner comfort that can be passed back to the client.

I learned this in early in my training. In a student clinic where low-income people came by referral, a young Salvadoran woman asked for help. On her first visit, she sat before me and immediately began a tale of abandonment at age 7, then years of living on the streets—in slavery, in forced prostitution, numerous rapes, beatings, and other traumas. One story followed another, followed another, followed another. I listened and listened. Her face talked, frozen in a permanent expression of despair.

I told my supervisor the problem. "She tells me the same stories over and over and over, and I don't know what to do."

"No," he answered. "She's not telling you the same stories. You're just having the same reaction over and over. She's overwhelmed, and now you're overwhelmed. Tell her to stop. And let her know it's because you need to slow down and take this at a rate that allows you to deal with it. This will allow her to slow down and do the same later. But first you have to be able to slow down and not get as overwhelmed as she is."

A community usually attends to the gang problem after an innocent person is killed in a drive-by shooting, or when something horrendous has occurred and politicians have to scramble to meet public demands for action. A frenzy of publicity, talk, promises, and grants surface to attention for a few weeks. Then the attention ebbs, and the gang members remain. We know gang problems won't be remedied by going into emergency mode continuously. Otherwise we are just reacting to the craziness, absorbing it, and dealing with it in a manner that is itself just as crazy.

Our communities need to settle down, take account of their resources, set their objectives, and start working toward them rationally and honestly. In time, each of our communities will come to understand the particular conditions that allow children to become marginalized and out of control. Each community will find its own method of counteracting them. I've given you some ideas in that direction.

Recovery from addictions remains elemental to eliminating violence and to the health of gang-involved children. But maintain your perspective, and take your time. It's a tough job, and if our efforts are to succeed, we have to do some groundwork first.

Final Thoughts

I had coffee one recent afternoon with a senior rabbi in Los Angeles. He told me that, as a child in South Africa, his father had died. He did not remember a funeral, and he was never taken to the tomb. He was dead, and the subject of the father became taboo in the house.

Within his orthodox community, all children had fathers, and he credits the absence of his own father for his decision to become a rabbi. If he could not have a father, nor even be allowed the memory of one, then he would become the ultimate father, the rabbi of the congregation.

Years later, when the rabbi's mother died, he went to the hospital to receive the death certificate. But the certificate read "divorced," not "widow," as it should have. The rabbi told me he then embarked on a long quest to find anyone alive who could explain the discrepancy.

The journey took him back to South Africa, to an old aunt who reminded him that, within the orthodox community, divorce brought shame on a family and almost never occurred. It was better to be dead than divorced. So for the sake of the family name and the children's reputation, it was decided that his father would disappear, the divorce explained as a death to the young children.

But the aunt also told him one more secret. The night he left, his father sat on the floor with his baggage and wept for hours. He would disappear from their lives because he knew the stigma divorce would bring. But he loved his children profoundly and continued to support them, although he would never see them again.

The rabbi told me that this revelation healed a wound he had carried his entire life. Even as an old man, the question of whether his father loved him still mattered to him.

All people hunger to know that they are prized. We want to hear the words, open the gift, receive the trophy in our hands. We crave the markers of acceptance, belonging, and approval. Like the rabbi, we all have a small child inside us who needs to know we are loved by those who are supposed to love us.

Gang members watch the news. It's on at six o'clock in their homes, just like in everyone else's. They know the world has decided they are the source of all its problems, and politicians are elected to fight a war against them, the violent gangsters. They respond with resentment to the hateful stares, the stack of trouble notes from teachers, the reprimands of judges and probation officers, the anger of parents who must constantly fetch them from detention. That's a lot of information telling a 15-year-old that he or she is no good.

And maybe, for the moment, this boy or girl is no good. Unfortunately, these gang members are still kids, and they still want us to love them. We're the adults, and we're supposed to. That's how kids tend to think. Rivera and Short (1968) conducted a study in which they observed the way in which community members talked to gang members and non-gang members. Their team found that adults in the community talked to the latter about the future: what their plans were, how school was going, if they had found jobs, what sports they were interested in. To gang members, community adults talked only about the immediate present: What are you doing here? How long have you been out of jail? What kind of trouble have you been causing? They never asked gang members about the future because community adults assumed they didn't have one.

This point is important. Yes, gang members are dangerous; yes, the destruction they cause makes us angry. It is not rational, it is not something to be talked out of, and it is certainly not a condition to be shamed out of.

Like other psychological difficulties, gang members' behavior can be changed, but only in the same way that alcoholism, codependence, and anorexia are dealt with: Time, patience, support, containment, monitoring, and the teaching of new skills. Maybe it makes you mad that it has to be that way: It's always maddening when people around us keep doing stupid things and we wish they would just stop. Stop drinking, stop starving yourself, stop going back to that awful husband, stop being so nervous all the time. Just stop it.

It doesn't work that way.

What I suggest, and the reason I have spent seven years writing this book, is that a solution to gang violence is possible and practical. People destroy themselves in lots of ways and for lots of reasons. But what works to halt that self-destruction tends to be the same no matter how one dresses up his or her particular form of suicide. Poor, minority children are human beings, made of the same stuff as the rest of us; and all we have learned about the difficult process of bringing psychological wellness to people applies to them as well.

One of the newer fields in psychology is the study of why some children are able to survive difficult environments while others perish. This is generally called the study of "risk and resiliency."

Researchers have found what one would expect: The more you have against you, the tougher time you're going to have. But Michael Rutter and Emmy Werner, two of the most prominent researchers in this field, have reached interesting conclusions. They have found that children who survive have visions of the world as a coherent, meaningful place. Life has a direction. It may be difficult, but there is a plan to follow. (Rutter 1976 and Werner 1982).

Viktor Frankl's work (1959) on the concentration camp experience said the same: The survivors were not the strongest physically, but those who were able to make sense of the day.

Psychologist B.F. Skinner's work with rats implied this in reverse: A rat would receive a shock as it sat still. The rat would jump, and where it landed it would receive another shock. When it moved back, it got another shock. The little rat soon discovered it had no place to go where it wouldn't receive pain, and what followed was self-mutilation, degeneration, and depression.

Children must have a sense of a coherent world. This can only come from an adult world that has a clear and insistent direction for them. In that regard, I conveyed to the kids at El Santo Niño a sense that they had a mission, that what they had to do was important and shouldn't be shortchanged. Their work had real value in a real world, and its completion would be noticed, important, and celebrated.

The powerful words in all of this are *plan, direction, coherence*—and one that Frankl, Rutter, and Werner all use in their own conclusions—*hope.*

We must remember that adults can sometimes muster hope by calling upon their reservoir of life experiences, but children do not have that luxury. They are still dependent upon us and cannot be talked into hopefulness when the adults who plan their future provide no basis for it.

We have created children willing to kill others, filled with addictions, looking forward to their own deaths. This is neither normal nor inevitable. It is a sign of severe neglect and of a breakdown in a community's function as a conduit to adulthood for its children. This is not a parental problem, but a parent-school-corrections-community problem. When, as a community of adults, we finally commit to seeing all our children to productive adulthood, and we are willing to stop blaming and instead start creating and collaborating, then we will take back our children.

Sugar Ray's advice will never fail us: It is always *how*, never *if.* There is always a how if we insist on finding it.

References

Frankl, V. (1959). *Man's Search for Meaning: An Introduction to Logotherapy.* Boston: Beacon Press.

Rivera, R.J., & Short, J.F. (1968). Significant adults, caretakers, and structures of opportunity: An exploratory study. In J.F. Short (Ed.), *Gang Delinquency and Delinquent Subcultures.* New York: Harper and Row.

Rutter, M. (1976). *Cycles of Disadvantage.* London: Heinemann Educational.

Werner, E. (1982). *Vulnerable But Invincible: A Longitudinal Study of Resilient Children and Youth.* New York: McGraw-Hill.

A Message
from the Author

The Salt River Pima-Maricopa Indian Community borders the cities of Scottsdale and Phoenix, Arizona. Their reservation was mandated in 1879 by President Rutherford B. Hayes, but the Pima and Maricopa have lived in this desert since time immemorial.

The Pima-Maricopa had ancient agrarian cultures, and the community supported itself through farming on the Salt River Reservation. This continued until the Colorado River was diverted to feed growing cities such as Los Angeles and Phoenix.

In addition to the diversion of the Salt River, a lack of employment, policies of the U.S. Bureau of Indian Affairs, European religions, and the forced education of tribal children in off-reservation schools have formed an onslaught that the Pima-Maricopa culture has not been able to withstand.

Currently, the Salt River Reservation is experiencing a gang problem severe enough to have attracted the attention of the national media. A significant factor in this problem is the absence of a comprehensive education system on the reservation itself.

In an effort to change this, the Pima-Maricopa have opened a new charter school to serve the Salt River community. But Desert Eagle High School can accommodate only 75 students, which means that hundreds of Pima-Maricopa children must be bused daily to the Mesa school district in Phoenix.

The key to any gang problem is an educational setting in which children feel valued and where viable adulthoods and identities become possible for even the most difficult students. What has impressed me most about Desert Eagle's efforts is reflected in the sentiments expressed by its students—gang members and those who are not—that here they feel at home, valued, and educated in a manner that instills pride in who they are as Native Americans. Many, particularly the gang-involved youth, have told me that Desert Eagle is the first school in which they feel truly wanted.

The Salt River community's goal is to enlarge and enrich Desert Eagle High School, allowing more tribal youth to be educated within their own community, where they can receive its values and attention. Although this is an expensive and difficult goal, especially in light of recent cuts in funding to Indian tribes, the Pima-Maricopa Indian Community is seeking and developing creative solutions.

For more information on the Pima-Maricopa Indian Community and its efforts to reown its children, contact the Pima-Maricopa Indian Community, c/o Desert Eagle High School, 10005 East Osborn Road, Scottsdale, AZ 85256; or send e-mail to saltriver@hotmail.com.

If you would like to contact me, you can do so through CWLA Press, 440 First Street NW, Third Floor, Washington, DC 20001-2085; 202/638-2952; FAX 202/638-4004; or send e-mail to books@cwla.org.

About the Author

Arturo Hernandez began working with gang members in his early teens when he joined a detention ministry so he could visit friends in juvenile hall. Since then, he has worked as a public school teacher, a school guidance counselor, a family therapist, and a consultant on juvenile delinquency and youth gang intervention, and has founded two experimental schools for gang-involved youth. He has lived and worked in East and South Central Los Angeles, Compton, and Watts, and among the rural gangs of the Salinas Valley. Currently a high school counselor and college professor in Los Angeles, he is nearing completion of a doctoral degree in educational psychology.

About the Artist

The cover art is an original work, specifically for *Peace in the Streets,* by Peter Tovar, an East Los Angeles artist. Known for his striking work with pastels and his involvement with Self-Help Graphics in Los Angeles, Tover is a long-term member of, and influence in, the Chicano art community.